Editor
Wanda Kelly

Managing Editor
Ina Massler Levin, M.A.

Editor-in-Chief
Sharon Coan, M.S. Ed.

Art Director
CJae Froshay

Art Coordinator
Denice Adorno

Cover Design
Lesley Palmer

Imaging
Rosa C. See

Production Manager
Phil Garcia

Publisher
Mary D. Smith, M.S. Ed.

Blake Staff

Editor
Sharon Dalgleish

Designed and typeset by
The Modern Art Production
Group

Printed by
Australian Print Group

372.61
C629r 75

HUBBARD BRANCH LIBRARY
12929 W. McNICHOLS
DETROIT, MI 48235
313-481-1752

D0800420

Grammar PRACTICE

Grades 5–6

Author
Peter Clutterbuck

This edition published by
Teacher Created Resources, Inc.
6421 Industry Way
Westminster, CA 92683
www.teachercreated.com
ISBN: 978-0-7439-3622-4

©2002 Teacher Created Resou
Reprinted, 200
Made in '
with permis
Blake Educ
Locked Bag 2
Glebe NSW 20

HUBBARD BRANCH LIBRARY
12929 W. McNICHOLS
DETROIT, MI 48235
313-481-1752

The classroom teacher may reproduce copies of materials in this book for classroom use only. The reproduction of any part for an entire school or school system is strictly prohibited. No part of this publication may be transmitted, stored, or recorded in any form without written permission from the publisher.

Contents

Contents *(cont.)*

Introduction

This third book of *Grammar Practice* for grades five and six provides teachers with resources, activities, and ideas aimed at consolidating and extending students' knowledge of grammar. The activity pages can be used as a resource around which to build and develop a classroom program.

Good grammar skills help children improve their expression and give them an appreciation of how the various elements of English are used to convey meaning. With an understanding of the rules, processes, and elements that govern English, children are able to communicate both correctly and effectively.

In the past, lessons in grammar often became irrelevant and meaningless to students because of the tendency to stress the elements rather than focus on the functions of the elements. *Grammar Practice* ensures that the functions of elements such as parts of speech, phrases, and sentences are related to expression in a practical and purposeful way.

Grammar Practice is designed to make it as easy as possible to find what you need. Photocopiable work sheets are grouped according to grammatical element, and each of these elements is introduced with a definition and examples for the teacher, followed by a collection of appropriate and motivating teaching strategies. With the three books in *Grammar Practice,* teachers can create an individual and comprehensive grammar program for their students.

How to Use This Book

The *Grammar Practice* series aims to improve children's ability to
* use language effectively in their own writing,
* use language accurately in their own writing,
* read critically the writing of others.

With this in mind, the books have been designed to make it easy for teachers to find the following:

The grammatical elements to teach at each level
* Refer to the overview provided by the assessment checklist.
* Read the background information to find the terminology and depth of treatment appropriate.

Concise background information about each grammatical element
* This is located in the introduction to each grammatical element.

Practical strategies showing how to teach each grammatical element
* Use activities as starting points to introduce a grammatical element and capture children's interest.
* Use other proven strategies to explicitly teach or model a grammatical element.
* Use games for reinforcement.

Blackline master (BLM) work sheets to reinforce learning
* They are a comprehensive resource around which to build a program.

Systematic teaching

Children need a solid general framework of grammatical understanding and skills to support their learning across the curriculum. To provide this framework, you may want to teach certain grammatical elements in a systematic way. The assessment checklists provided in each level of *Grammar Practice* indicate the grammatical elements that students should understand by the end of each level. The checklists can be used to program your systematic teaching and to record children's achievements.

Incidental teaching

Incidental teaching is an important strategy to use to help students build on prior learning and develop their understanding of grammar in context. A grammar lesson might, therefore, stem from the context of different texts children are reading and writing or from the need to deal with a specific problem individual children or groups of children are experiencing in their own writing. To teach at this point of need, simply dip into *Grammar Practice* and find the appropriate information, strategies, or work sheets for your children.

Assessment

To be successful, any grammar program must be accompanied by regular assessment. The methods used may differ from teacher to teacher but should encompass the basic points.

For each student, assessment should accomplish the following:

(a) record clearly the progress being made;

(b) indicate the future steps being planned for reinforcement and extension;

(c) indicate specific areas of difficulty and possible remediation;

(d) use various strategies to determine whether an outcome has been achieved;

(e) be a relevant and careful measurement of the stage of grammar development;

(f) provide clear and precise suggestions to parents as to how they may best assist at home;

(g) provide clear and precise information to teachers.

Assessment Checklist

Name _____ Quarter

Parts of Speech	1	2	3	4
Understands, identifies and uses correctly				
different types of nouns, including abstract				
action, saying, thinking, and being and having verbs				
tenses				
subject/verb agreement				
different types of adjectives				
a variety of adverbs				
degrees of comparison				
definite and indefinite articles				
prepositions as place words				
personal, possessive, and relative pronouns				
conjunctions and connecting words				
Sentences				
Identifies				
subject, verb, and object				
phrases and clauses				
dependency of one clause on another				
Identifies and writes				
simple, compound, and complex sentences				
direct speech and indirect speech				
adverbial phrases and adjectival phrases				
Punctuation				
Uses				
capital letters				
periods, question marks				
commas, semicolons, colons, dashes				
apostrophes				
question marks in direct speech				

Comments

Areas of strength/difficulty _____

Steps being undertaken to reinforce areas of difficulty or extend grammar skills

_____

Parts of Speech

Every name is called a **noun**,
As *fence* and *flower*, *street* and *town*;

In place of noun the **pronoun** stands,
As *he* and *she* can raise their hands;

The **adjective** describes a thing,
As *magic* wand and *twisted* string;

The **verb** means action, something done—
To *read* and *write*, to *jump* and *run*;

How things are done the **adverbs** tell,
As *quickly*, *slowly*, *badly*, *well*;

The **preposition** shows the place,
As *in* the street or *at* the base;

Conjunctions join, in many ways,
Sentences, words, *or* phrase *and* phrase.

anonymous

Nouns

Introduction

Fifth and sixth grade students should be familiar with the following functions of **nouns**.

(a) Nouns are the **names** of things around us. Nouns that are used to name general things (rather than a particular person or thing) are called **common nouns**.

Examples: *dog*   *table*   *car*   *bottle*

(b) Some nouns are the names of particular or special people or things. These are called **proper nouns** and are written with a capital letter at the beginning.

Example: *Mr. Rogers stayed at the Hilton Hotel in San Francisco last July.*

(c) Some nouns are the names we use for collections of things. These are called **collective nouns**.

Examples:

a *flock* of birds   a *herd* of cattle   a *bunch* of grapes

a *smack* of jellyfish   a *siege* of herons   a *murder* of ravens

an *army* of frogs   a *charm* of finches   a *pod* of dolphins

Other collective nouns name a number of different things in the same class.

Examples: *fruit*   *tools*   *luggage*   *birds*

Children often have difficulty deciding whether a collective noun is singular or plural.

- Words that represent a number of different things in the same group always take a singular verb.

  Examples: *furniture is*   *luggage is*   *linen is*

- Words that have a plural meaning but no plural form take a plural verb.

  Examples: *people are*   *police are*

- Other collective nouns can take a plural verb if the context emphasis is on a group of individuals. However, the singular is preferred.

  Examples: *The crowd is cheering.*
  Congress is in session.
  The crew is ready.
  The Olympic Games are in Salt Lake City.

Nouns (cont.)

(d) Nouns can be **singular** or **plural**. The relevant plural constructions at this level are the following:

- Many plurals are made by simply adding *-s*.
  Examples: *dog/dogs*   *girl/girls*

- If the noun ends in *-s, -sh, -ch,* or *-x*, make the plural by adding *-es*.
  Examples: *bus/buses*   *bush/bushes*
  fox/foxes   *church/churches*

- If the noun ends in a *-y* before which there is a consonant, make the plural by changing *-y* to *-i* and adding *-es*.
  Examples: *fairy/fairies*   *city/cities*

- If the noun ends in *-y* before which there is a vowel (*a, e, i, o, u*), make the plural by simply adding *-s*.
  Examples: *monkey/monkeys*   *toy/toys*

- If the noun ends in *-f*, change the *-f to -v* and add *-es*.
  Examples: *loaf/loaves*   *leaf/leaves*

  However, some simply add *-s*.
  Examples: *roof/roofs*   *chief/chiefs*

- Some nouns have irregular plurals.
  Examples: *foot/feet*   *goose/geese*
  man/men   *child/children*

(e) **Possessive nouns** are especially difficult for children at this level to grasp.

- The possessive of a singular noun is formed by adding an *apostrophe* and *-s* at the end of the word. No letters are changed or left off the original word.
  Examples: the *boy's* dog (The boy owns a dog.)
  the *lady's* car (The lady owns a car.)

- The possessive of a plural noun ending in *-s* is formed by adding an *apostrophe*.
  Examples: horses/*horses'* manes   ladies/*ladies'* cars

- The possessive of a plural noun not ending in *-s* is formed by adding an *apostrophe* and *-s*.
  Examples: children/*children's*   men/*men's*

(f) **Terms of address** are the nouns we use when we refer to or address certain people.
  Examples: *Mr.* Jones   *Ms.* Smith   *Doctor* Smith   *Captain* Peters

Nouns (cont.)

(g) An **abstract noun** is the name of something that can't be recognized by the five senses—you can't touch, taste, hear, smell, or see it—it can only be recognized by the mind.

Examples:
courage	*misery*	*delight*	*fear*
excitement	*distress*	*hope*	*possibility*

Children should also be introduced to the relationship of nouns to words such as verbs (words that tell what the nouns are doing), adjectives (words that describe the nouns), and pronouns (words that take the places of nouns).

Teaching Strategies

Alphabet game
Challenge students to write a common noun for every letter of the alphabet. These could be related to a particular topic or theme, for example, the earth, cities, or endangered species. Make the challenge more exciting by adding a time limit. Students could then repeat the activity with proper nouns.

Labels
Have children draw a diagram (for example, of a car, bicycle, or horse) and then add labels.

Lists
Have children make lists of nouns, such as Things I Need to Take to Camp or Things I Might See in New York City.

Mystery nouns
Children can describe a mystery object and challenge classmates to guess what it is.
I am a sphere.
I am made of glass.
You play games with me.
(marble)

Puzzles
Have children make anagram or jumbled letter puzzles for their classmates to solve.
flow = wolf   *arrtoc (vegetable) = carrot*

Abstract opposites
Have children provide the opposite words for abstract nouns you read aloud.
love/hate
beauty/ugliness

Nouns (cont.)

Cloze

Create cloze exercises by selecting an extract from a story and blotting out the nouns. Have children add nouns that maintain the context of the story.

Proper noun match

Read aloud a list of common nouns. Have children supply a proper noun for each.

planet/Venus

country/Iceland

river/Mississippi

Lots of

Read aloud a sentence which includes the words "lots of." Have children suggest a suitable collective noun.

I saw lots of birds.

I saw lots of cars.

Unusual collections

Encourage children to explore collective nouns that are not so well known. Encyclopedias and dictionaries will assist them.

Made-up collections

After discussing common collective nouns (a flock of birds, a herd of cattle), have students make up their own imaginary collective nouns that they think would suit a group of creatures.

a slither of snakes   *a hop of frogs*

a gathering of goannas   *a trumpet of elephants*

Abstract mime

Write abstract nouns on slips of paper and place the papers in a hat. Allow children to pick a paper from the hat and mime the abstract noun. The rest of the class must guess the abstract noun.

happiness

sadness

anger

kindness

WORD BANK

Common Nouns

airplane	daughter	nephew	soup
aunt	dentist	newspaper	sugar
bridge	doctor	niece	teacher
captain	holiday	ocean	tunnel
castle	husband	person	valley
coach	island	piano	village
country	music	pupil	whale
creek	neighbor	rooster	women

Proper Nouns

Aunt Tanya
the Big Apple
Captain Clancy
Christmas
Christmas Day
December
Doctor Smith
Easter
the Empire State Building
Long Island

Collective Nouns

army	fleet
band	flight
bed	flotilla
bunch	gang
class	herd
colony	litter
company	pack
congregation	pride
covey	swarm
crowd	team

Abstract Nouns

anger	distress	honor	love
beauty	excitement	hope	misery
consideration	fear	idea	pity
courage	friendship	imagination	pleasure
danger	fun	joy	possibility
delight	gladness	kindness	prettiness
despair	greed	laughter	sadness
dismay	happiness	loneliness	shame

Common Nouns

Name _____ Grammar BLM **1**

Nouns that are used to name general things are called common nouns.

1. **Sort the nouns in the box under the headings below.**

knees	yachting	caviar	biscuits
steak	bacon	stomach	football
tennis	cap	jacket	veins
sweater	skull	hockey	trousers

Clothing	Body	Food	Sport

2. **Choose from the box the word that names each group of things.**

a. falcon, emu, dove _____

b. stool, desk, table _____

c. badminton, golf, soccer _____

d. truck, bus, car _____

e. orchid, daisy, pansy _____

f. currants, cherries, apricots _____

g. herring, flounder, cod _____

h. spaniels, terriers, poodles _____

sports
flowers
birds
dogs
furniture
fish
vehicles
fruit

3. **Circle in each row the noun that is out of place.**

a. butterfly grasshopper thistle wasp

b. walrus palm olive maple

c. panther lion tiger zebra

d. lettuce apricot carrot onion

e. attic cellar kitchen stomach

f. planet doctor nurse surgeon

Common Nouns

Name _____ Grammar BLM **2**

Nouns that are used to name general things are called common nouns.

1. **Find the nouns in the grid. Write each one beside its meaning.**

r	t	t	r	o	u	t	b
a	i	p	e	a	c	h	r
v	g	o	n	i	o	n	a
e	e	p	a	n	s	y	s
n	r	l	o	u	s	e	s
s	k	u	l	l	x	z	p
b	r	e	a	d	y	t	v

a. body part _____

b. insect _____

c. fruit _____

d. fish _____

e. bird _____

f. large cat _____

g. metal _____

h. flower _____

i. vegetable _____

j. food _____

2. **Color the boxes that contain words that can be used as nouns.**

barrel	falcon	bugle	leather	vinegar
happy	silly	orchid	sofa	canal
eel	pitcher	chewing	dirty	tall
old	silk	hamper	ferret	envelope

3. **Choose 5 nouns from question 2. Write a sentence using each one.**

a. _____

b. _____

c. _____

d. _____

e. _____

Collective Nouns

Name _____

Collective nouns are the names we use for collections of things.

1. Use a collective noun from the box to fill each space.

> brood   fleet   library   litter   tuft   flight   batch   bunch

a. a _____ of aircraft

b. a _____ of cakes

c. a _____ of grass

d. a _____ of grapes

e. a _____ of ships

f. a _____ of puppies

g. a _____ of chickens

h. a _____ of books

2. Add a collective noun from the box to complete each sentence.

> bouquet   hail   gaggle   pride   staff   plague

a. On our farm we have a _____ geese.

b. The gangster dropped in a _____ of bullets.

c. The bride carried a _____ of flowers.

d. A _____ of grasshoppers devoured the lawn.

e. A _____ of lions dozed under the trees.

f. My mom's company has a large _____ .

3. Add a collective noun of your own on each line below.

a. a _____ of swimmers

b. a _____ of eggs

c. a _____ of sheep

d. a _____ of sailors

e. a _____ of hay

f. a _____ of wool

g. a _____ of trees

h. a _____ of bananas

Proper Nouns

Name _____   Grammar BLM

Proper nouns are the names of particular people, places, or things. They are written with a capital letter at the beginning.

1. Write the proper noun from the box beside the matching common noun below.

| September   Nile   Tuesday   Henry Hudson   Miami   Japan |

a. country _____   d. river _____

b. month _____   e. day _____

c. explorer _____   f. city _____

2. Use the proper nouns in the box to complete the story.

| Vanessa   Monday   Long Beach   April
| Good Friday   Tony   San Francisco   California   Seahawk |

On _____ the eighth of _____ , two students, a girl named

_____ and a boy named _____ , left the seaside city

of _____ in _____ to sail a yacht named _____ down

the coast to _____ . They arrived safely on _____ , much to the

relief of their parents.

3. Write the word from the box that names each group of proper nouns.

| months
| oceans
| planets
| countries
| states
| mountains |

a. Chile, Canada, England _____

b. June, August, July _____

c. Saturn, Uranus, Neptune _____

d. Everest, Kosciusko, Kilimanjaro _____

e. Pacific, Atlantic, Indian _____

f. Florida, Maine, Oregon _____

Plural Nouns

Singular nouns refer to one person, place, or thing. Plural nouns refer to more than one person, place, or thing.

1. **Write the plural of the word in parentheses. Hint: If there is a vowel before the *y*, add *s*. If there is a consonant before the *y*, change the *y* to *i* and add *es*.**

   a. All the children in our school were given _____. (journal)

   b. There are lots of large _____ in the United States. (city)

   c. The _____ were making a lot of noise. (turkey)

   d. This supermarket has over five hundred _____. (cart)

   e. We ate all the _____ on the tree. (cherry)

   f. Lots of _____ gathered around the rotten food. (fly)

2. **Write the plural of each word. Hint: For some words that end in *f*, change the *f* to *v* and add *es*. For others, simply add *s*.**

   a. loaf _____   e. leaf _____

   b. chief _____   f. handkerchief _____

   c. knife _____   g. thief _____

   d. half _____   h. wolf _____

3. **Write the plural of the word in parentheses.**

   a. The two _____ decided to end the war. (army)

   b. They read the story *Snow White and the Seven* _____. (Dwarf)

   c. When the box was dropped, all the _____ broke. (glass)

   d. At the zoo we saw lots of _____. (monkey)

   e. Several _____ were needed to pull the wagon. (ox)

   f. The _____ left their coats on the bed. (lady)

Plural Nouns

Singular nouns refer to one person, place, or thing. Plural nouns refer to more than one person, place, or thing.

1. **Write the plural of the word in parentheses. Hint: Most nouns form the plural by adding _s_. Those that end in _ch, sh, s_, or _x_ add _es_.**

   a. There are over seven _____ in our town. (**church**)

   b. There are lots of _____ growing in the playground. (**tree**)

   c. The frightened dog hid between the two _____ . (**bush**)

   d. Jan put all the _____ on the table. (**box**)

   e. My brother ate three _____ for lunch. (**peach**)

   f. The six school _____ were in a line. (**bus**)

2. **Write the plural of each of the following words. Hint: They are all irregular.**

   a. goose _____   e. tooth _____

   b. man _____   f. woman _____

   c. foot _____   g. child _____

   d. louse _____   h. mouse _____

3. **Write the plural of the word in parentheses. Hint: Some nouns that end in _o_ add _es_ to make the plural. Others simply add _s_.**

   a. We planted _____ in the garden. (**potato**)

   b. On our holiday, Kyle took lots of _____ . (**photo**)

   c. South America has many _____ . (**volcano**)

   d. Hundreds of _____ were bathing in the pool. (**hippo**)

   e. The brave _____ were all given medals. (**hero**)

   f. I sliced the three _____ to make a salad. (**tomato**)

Forming Nouns

Name _____   Grammar BLM **7**

Nouns can be formed from other parts of speech.

1. Complete the sentence by making a noun from the word in parentheses.

a. We placed an _____ in the newspaper. (**advertise**)

b. The _____ took place in a nearby church. (**marry**)

c. Our teacher asked for our daily _____ . (**attend**)

d. Ian's _____ has been much better this quarter. (**behave**)

e. They had to make an important _____ . (**decide**)

f. The teacher gave us a lot of _____ . (**encourage**)

2. Complete the sentence by making a noun from the word in parentheses.

a. It was with great _____ we said goodbye. (**sad**)

b. The firefighter was awarded for her _____ . (**brave**)

c. We sat in the _____ of the shade. (**cool**)

d. There was a lot of _____ between the two teams. (**bitter**)

e. We gasped at the _____ of the mountains. (**beautiful**)

f. We were not sure what _____ he was suffering from. (**sick**)

3. Make nouns from each of the words below.

a. punish   a severe _____

b. invent   a clever _____

c. friendly   a good _____

d. appear   an untidy _____

e. weigh   a heavy _____

f. lose   a sad _____

Possessive Nouns

An apostrophe is used to show possession (that something belongs to something or someone).

- **For a singular noun add an *apostrophe* and *s* at the end of the word.**
  the horse's mane
  the child's toys
- **For a plural noun add an *apostrophe* if the word ends in *s***
  (*the horses' manes*)
  or an *apostrophe* and *s* if the word does not end in *s*
  (*the children's toys*).

1. **Rewrite the following to show possession.**

   a. the dress of the girl _____

   b. the stripes of the tiger _____

   c. the pencil of the boy _____

   d. the handbags of the lady _____

   e. the leaves of the tree _____

   f. the petals of the flower _____

   g. the antics of the clown _____

   h. the uniform of the police officer _____

2. **Now rewrite the following to show possession.**

   a. the dresses of the girls _____

   b. the ears of the donkeys _____

   c. the books of the men _____

   d. the saddles of the horses _____

   e. the houses of the women _____

   f. the pencils of the boys _____

   g. the nests of the birds _____

   h. the ship of the sailors _____

Abstract Nouns

An abstract noun is the name of something that can't be recognized by the five senses. You can't touch, taste, hear, smell, or see it—it can only be recognized by the mind.

1. **Add an abstract noun from the box to fill each space.**

> excitement   fun   pain   health   length   happiness   care   wealth

   a. We had lots of _____ at the show.

   b. After he fell over, Tom had a _____ in his leg.

   c. Although he has been ill, he is in good _____ now.

   d. There was a lot of _____ when the mouse escaped.

   e. I am not sure of the _____ of this rope.

   f. Mr. Richman thinks that _____ is important.

   g. The genie said that I would have health, wealth, and _____ .

   h. Tim took a lot of _____ with his work.

2. **Find the abstract nouns in this grid. Write them on the lines.**

s	a	d	n	e	s	s
g	s	o	r	r	o	w
r	g	r	i	e	f	g
e	l	p	a	i	n	l
e	o	f	e	a	r	e
d	v	j	o	y	x	e
x	e	a	n	g	e	r

_____   _____

_____   _____

_____   _____

_____   _____

3. **Write an abstract noun to suit each situation. Compare your answers with those of a friend.**

   a. Your younger brother scribbles all over your new book. _____

   b. Your teacher tells you there is no school next week. _____

   c. You have played sports all day. _____

   d. A poisonous spider lands on your arm. _____

Verbs

Introduction

Fifth and sixth grade students should understand the following types of **verbs** and their uses.

(a) **Action verbs** are words that express concrete actions. They are common in spoken and written language at all levels of use.

Examples: *eat*   *sit*   *run*   *work*   *jump*

(b) **Saying verbs** express spoken actions.

Examples: *talk*   *tell*   *say*   *yell*   *suggest*

(c) **Thinking and feeling verbs** express actions that happen mentally, such as feelings, ideas, thoughts, or attitudes.

Examples: I *like* Sam.   Katy *believed* the story.

(d) **Being and having verbs** tell us about what things are and what they have. The verb "to be" is the English language's most irregular and most important verb. It is used as an independent verb and is also the most commonly used auxiliary verb.

Examples: Ben *is* a bowler.   Ali *has* answers.

(e) **Auxiliary or helping verbs** are used with main verbs. The auxiliary verb and the main verb become a **verb phrase**. Some common auxiliary verbs are *do*, *can*, *may*, *must*, and *should*.

Examples: Gail *is riding.*   Gail *has been riding.*

Verbs not only express actions but also tell us the time of the action. The tense of a verb tells us when the action is, was, or will be carried out. There are six tenses used in English.

The three simple tenses are past, present, and future.

(a) **Present tense** refers to actions that are happening now, at this moment.

Example: I *like* the chocolate flavor.

(b) **Past tense** refers to actions that happened in the past, seconds or years ago.

Example: I *liked* the chocolate flavor.

(c) **Future tense** refers to actions which will happen in the future, in seconds or years.

Example: I *will like* the chocolate flavor.

Verbs *(cont.)*

The three perfect tenses are present perfect, past perfect, and future perfect.

(a) **Present perfect** refers to action that is complete at the time of writing or speaking. It is formed by combining the auxiliary *have* or *has* with the past participle of the verb.

Example: I *have liked* the chocolate flavor.

(b) **Past perfect** refers to action that was completed before some specific time in the past. It is formed by combining the auxiliary *had* with the past participle.

Example: I *had liked* the chocolate flavor until I became ill.

(c) **Future perfect** refers to actions that will be completed at a specific time in the future. It is formed by combining the auxiliary *will have* with the past participle.

Example: I *will have liked* the chocolate flavor for ten years by May.

Regular verbs form the past tense and past participle by adding *-ed* or *-d* to the present tense form. Sometimes the *-ed* or *-d* changes to *-t*.

Examples: *call, called, called*   *build, built, built*

Irregular verbs do not simply add *-ed* to form the past tense and past participle. The word itself changes form—and these changes have to be learned.

Examples: *steal, stole, stolen*   *swim, swam, swum*

A verb can be **active or passive voice**. Voice indicates whether the subject of the sentence is acting or receiving the action of the verb. Passive voice always includes a form of the auxiliary verb "to be" (I am/was/will be/have been/had been/will have been) and the past participle of the main verb.

Examples: *active*   *passive*

           Katy *read* the book.   The book *was read* by Katy.

Fifth and sixth grade students should know that **a verb must agree with its subject in person and number**. If the subject is singular, the verb must be singular; if the subject is plural, the verb must be plural. If the subject is in the first person, second person, or third person, the verb must also be in that person.

Examples:	*singular*	*plural*
1st person	*I like chocolate.*	*We like chocolate.*
2nd person	*You like chocolate.*	*You like chocolate.*
3rd person	*He/she/it likes chocolate.*	*They like chocolate.*

- A compound subject requires a plural verb form.
  Example: Here come the bride and groom.

- Collective nouns usually require singular verb forms.
  Example: The pod of whales could be seen from the shore.

Verbs (cont.)

Teaching Strategies

Puzzle verbs
On the chalkboard write the first letter of a verb and then a dash for each remaining letter. Tell the class what the verb means. Have volunteers add the missing letters.

g _ _ _ _ _   *to run like a horse (gallop)*
w _ _ _   *to cry (weep)*

Verb lists
Spend time encouraging students to seek out and use the most suitable verb at all times. This can be done by simple exercises on the chalkboard.
The frightened rabbit ran to its hole.
Have children replace *ran* with more effective verbs.
bolted   hopped   shot   leaped

Charades
Have children act out roles while others guess what they are doing.
You are drying the dishes.

Mixed-up verbs
Have children add suitable verbs to given nouns.
Dogs bark.   Cats purr.
They can then mix them up in a humorous way and create cartoons.
Fish bark.   Dogs fly.

Make it active
Have children identify verbs in a sentence and state whether they are in the active or passive voice.
Tom read the newspaper.
The newspaper was read by Tom.
Have children change sentences from the passive to the active voice.

In the past
Provide plenty of practice for children in the use of the past tense and past participles, especially of irregular verbs. These can be short oral activities.
I drive my car.   Yesterday I _____ my car.
I have _____ my car.

I think . . .
Encourage children to orally state opinions on certain topics. Remind them to use thinking and feeling verbs.
I believe that . . .
It seems that . . .
As children become more confident, conduct panel games or simple debates.

WORD BANK

Verbs

Action Verbs

build
climb
dawdle
hurtle
knock
leave
meander
shuffle
trundle
waddle

Saying Verbs

chuckle
exclaim
growl
howl
laugh
moan
roar
shriek
sigh
wail

Thinking/Feeling Verbs

believe
dislike
feel
know
prefer
seem
suppose
think
understand
wonder

Irregular Verbs

Present Tense	Past Tense	Past Participle (have/has/had)
become	became	become
begin	began	begun
come	came	come
do	did	done
drive	drove	driven
eat	ate	eaten
fly	flew	flown
forget	forgot	forgotten
go	went	gone
hang (picture)	hung	hung
hang (person)	hanged	hanged
know	knew	known
lay (to place/put)	laid	laid
lie (to recline)	lay	lain
lie (tell falsehood)	lied	lied
ride	rode	ridden
rise	rose	risen
see	saw	seen
sneak	sneaked	sneaked
write	wrote	written

Verbs

Action verbs express an action we can see, for example, *work, run, sit.*

1. **Circle the action verb in each sentence.**

   a. The dog bit the postman.

   b. Ian listened carefully.

   c. The teacher tapped the table with his ruler.

   d. Susan read a book about dinosaurs.

   e. The dog ate the old bone.

   f. We wandered through the rain forest.

2. **Use a verb from the box to fill each space.**

   | pounced   scowled   searched   pruned   wiped   gushed |

   a. When we turned the tap, the water _____ out.

   b. The angry lady _____ at me.

   c. The hungry cat _____ on the mouse.

   d. After he finished the ice cream, he _____ his face.

   e. The farmer _____ the fruit trees.

   f. We _____ everywhere but could not find the missing watch.

3. **What does each do?**

   | leaps   gambols   gallops   slithers |
   | scampers   soars   waddles   struts |

   a. A snake _____ .   e. A rooster _____ .

   b. A horse _____ .   f. A duck _____ .

   c. A lamb _____ .   g. An eagle _____ .

   d. A frog _____ .   h. A mouse _____ .

Verbs

Name _____   Grammar BLM **11**

Action verbs express an action we can see, for example, *work, run, sit*.

1. Circle the action verb in each sentence.

   a. The builders constructed the new home.

   b. We grilled the sausages on the barbecue.

   c. Heavy rain fell on the roof last night.

   d. The mechanic removed the nuts from the bolts.

   e. Sally wrote a letter to her friend.

   f. The acrobats performed some amazing stunts.

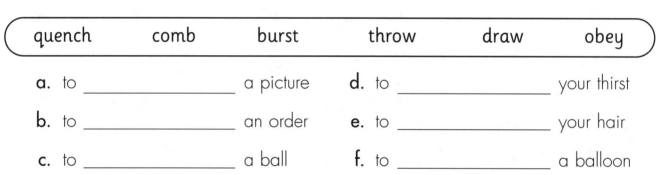

2. Use a verb from the box to fill each space.

quench	comb	burst	throw	draw	obey

   a. to _____ a picture   **d.** to _____ your thirst

   b. to _____ an order   **e.** to _____ your hair

   c. to _____ a ball   **f.** to _____ a balloon

3. Add an action verb of your own to complete each sentence. Then think of a different action verb to give the sentence a different meaning.

   a. The cat _____ its tail.   The cat _____ its tail.

   b. The ball _____ the window.   The ball _____ the window.

   c. Dad _____ the dishes.   Dad _____ the dishes.

   d. The car _____ the oily road.   The car _____ the oily road.

Verbs

Action verbs express an action we can see, for example, *work, run, sit.*

1. Sort the action verbs under the headings.

serving	studying	lobbing	browsing
roasting	acing	cleaning	cooking
researching	peeling	reading	volleying

at a tennis match	in the library	in the kitchen
_____	_____	_____
_____	_____	_____
_____	_____	_____
_____	_____	_____

2. Circle the action verb in the parentheses.

a. The dog went straight out to (bury berry) the bone.

b. They tried to (pier peer) through the curtains.

c. The rocket (mist missed) its target.

d. It is rude to (stair stare) at other people.

e. Water supplies began to (lessen lesson) during the drought.

3. Unjumble the letters in parentheses and write the action verb in the space.

a. Tomorrow the chickens should _____ from the eggs. (ahtch)

b. I was lucky the wasp did not _____ me. (ingst)

c. You must now _____ the clothes. (awsh)

d. Be sure your little brother does not _____ that toy. (wsallow)

e. The dog did not _____ the fence. (umjp)

Verbs

Saying verbs express a spoken action, for example, *talk, tell, said.*

1. **Circle the saying verb in each sentence.**

   a. Sally talked to the new boy.
   b. Tom yelled at the dog that was eating his pie.
   c. "I will be late," said Ben.
   d. The children chatted for a long time before going to sleep.
   e. The teacher asked the class to get back to work.
   f. They screamed when the Big Dipper suddenly dropped back to Earth.

2. **Add a saying verb of your own to each sentence.**

   a. The boy _____ as he ran down the street.

   b. She _____ as she slipped on the wet floor.

   c. Grade six _____ when they were told they had raised the most

      money.

   d. The children _____ as they slid down the water slide.

   e. The cat _____ as she ran towards her dish of food.

   f. The angry mother _____, "Clean up your room!"

3. **What noise does each make?**

grunts	trumpets	chirps	bellows
brays	bleats	screeches	gobbles

   a. A lamb _____ .   e. A pig _____ .

   b. A turkey _____ .   f. An elephant _____ .

   c. A parrot _____ .   g. A sparrow _____ .

   d. A donkey _____ .   h. A bull _____ .

Verbs

Thinking verbs express actions that happen mentally, such as feelings, ideas, thoughts or attitudes; for example, I *like* **Sam.**

1. **Circle the thinking verb in each sentence.**

    a. I believed the story.

    b. I think people should recycle.

    c. I wondered what would happen next.

    d. Tom thought about it for awhile.

    e. I understand what you mean.

    f. Christopher enjoyed the movie.

2. **Change the noun in parentheses to a thinking verb.**

    a. His behavior _____ me. (**anger**)

    b. The principal was _____ by the graffiti. (**sadness**)

    c. I was _____ by the story. (**amazement**)

    d. The new boy _____ about his achievements. (**boastfulness**)

    e. I _____ that we should leave at four o'clock. (**agreement**)

    f. I _____ being forced to eat my vegetables. (**hatred**)

3. **Write your thoughts and feelings on an issue that is important to you. Then circle all the thinking and feeling verbs you used.**

    _____

    _____

    _____

    _____

    _____

Verbs

Being and having verbs tell us about what things are and what they have; for example, *Ben is a bowler.* When forms of the verbs "to be" and "to have" are joined with other main verbs, they become auxiliary or helping verbs; for example, *Gail is riding.* (Together the auxiliary verb and the main verb become a verb phrase. In the example, *is riding* becomes the verb phrase.)

1. Circle the being or having verb in each sentence.

   a. Max has a bad cold.
   b. Ali is the best speller.
   c. The books are here.
   d. Nick was there a minute ago.
   e. I am the captain of the team.
   f. I have the string.

2. Underline the main verb and circle the auxiliary verb in each sentence.

   a. I am going to the movies tonight.
   b. Mom is painting the house this weekend.
   c. The teacher was helping us.
   d. Tom will run in the race.
   e. Our class has read that book.
   f. I have seen a shooting star.

3. Use three of the being and having verbs from number 1 in sentences of your own.

   _____

   _____

   _____

4. Use three of the verb phrases (auxiliary verb plus main verb) from number 2 in sentences of your own.

   _____

   _____

   _____

Verb Tense

The tense of a verb tells us when the action is, was, or will be carried out. Present tense refers to actions that are happening now, at this moment. Past tense refers to actions that happened in the past, a few seconds ago or years ago. Future tense refers to actions that will happen in the future, in a few seconds or in a few years.

Present tense:	She *likes* the chocolate flavor.
Past tense:	She *liked* the chocolate flavor.
Future tense:	She *will like* the chocolate flavor.

1. Change each of the words in the box to the past tense verb. Then use the past tense verbs to complete the sentences. Hint: Some words add *-ed* to make the past tense.

> delight ___   defeat ___   bark ___   thank ___   start ___   walk ___

   a. I _____ the teacher for helping me throughout the year.

   b. The dog _____ loudly at the stranger.

   c. Our football team _____ the other team 10–3.

   d. I was _____ when I was told I had won the prize.

   e. We _____ over three miles to the nearest house.

   f. The concert _____ right on time.

2. Change each of the words in the box to the past tense verb. Then use the past tense verbs to complete the sentences. Hint: If the word ends in *-e*, add *-d* to make the past tense.

> whistle ___   refuse ___   waste ___   describe ___   capture ___   continue ___

   a. The hunters _____ the leopard in the net.

   b. The soldier _____ to obey the orders of her sergeant.

   c. The children _____ a lot of good food.

   d. He _____ loudly to call his dog.

   e. The witness _____ the thief to the police officer.

   f. Although her leg hurt badly, Freya _____ in the race.

Verb Tense

The tense of a verb tells us when the action is, was, or will be carried out. Present tense refers to actions that are happening now, at this moment. Past tense refers to actions that happened in the past, a few seconds ago or years ago. Future tense refers to actions that will happen in the future, in a few seconds or in a few years.

Present tense:	She *likes* the chocolate flavor.
Past tense:	She *liked* the chocolate flavor.
Future tense:	She *will like* the chocolate flavor.

1. Write the past tense verbs on the lines. Hint: If the word ends in *-y*, change the *-y* to *-i* and add *-ed* to make the past tense.

   a. study _____   e. terrify _____

   b. deny _____   f. tidy _____

   c. multiply _____   g. copy _____

   d. bury _____   h. hurry _____

2. Use the past tense verbs from number 1 to complete the sentences.

   a. The dog _____ its bone in the garden.

   b. When I _____ two by four I got eight.

   c. The thief _____ stealing the jewels.

   d. Sally _____ hard to pass her spelling test.

   e. The savage dog _____ the young child.

   f. I _____ up the living room for my mother.

   g. Mike _____ the address for Peter.

   h. Joanne _____ to school because she thought she was late.

Verb Tense

The tense of a verb tells us when the action is, was, or will be carried out. Present tense refers to actions that are happening now, at this moment. Past tense refers to actions that happened in the past, a few seconds ago or years ago. Future tense refers to actions that will happen in the future, in a few seconds or in a few years.

Present tense:	She *likes* the chocolate flavor.
Past tense:	She *liked* the chocolate flavor.
Future tense:	She *will like* the chocolate flavor.

1. Complete the sentences by writing the past tense of the verb in parentheses. Hint: Some verbs form the past tense by doubling the final letter and adding *-ed*.

    a. The car _____ across the oily road. (**skid**)

    b. The old man _____ for money to buy food. (**beg**)

    c. The glass broke when he _____ it on the floor. (**drop**)

    d. The thieves _____ the hotel last night. (**rob**)

    e. Peter _____ his sister a woolen sweater. (**knit**)

    f. I _____ in the sugar before I drank the tea. (**stir**)

    g. The class _____ to Chicago by train. (**travel**)

    h. The leaking faucet _____ all night. (**drip**)

2. Use the past tense verbs of the words in the box to complete the story. Hint: Some verbs change their spelling to make the past tense. You might need to say the verb aloud to see if it sounds right.

ride	speak	tell	bring	ring	teach	get	eat	go	fly

Yesterday Tim _____ his bike to school. When he arrived he _____ to Lisa and _____ her he had _____ his kite to school. At nine o'clock he _____ the bell. In class the teacher _____ the children how to do long division. At recess Tim _____ a delicious cake from his lunchbox and _____ it. Then he _____ out onto the playground where he _____ his kite.

Verb Tense

Name _____

The tense of a verb tells us when the action is, was, or will be carried out. Present tense refers to actions that are happening now, at this moment. Past tense refers to actions that happened in the past, a few seconds ago or years ago. Future tense refers to actions that will happen in the future, in a few seconds or in a few years.

Present tense:	She *likes* the chocolate flavor.
Past tense:	She *liked* the chocolate flavor.
Future tense:	She *will like* the chocolate flavor.

1. Underline all the present and past tense verbs. Then rewrite each joke in the future tense.

   a. What do people make in a clock factory? They make faces all day.

   _____

   b. Why did the cross-eyed teacher quit? He couldn't control his pupils.

   _____

   c. What went over the tongue and through the eye? A shoelace did.

   _____

   d. Why was the exterminator so sad? He couldn't bear to see the moth bawl.

   _____

   e. What did one eye say to the other eye? "Between you and me, something smells."

   _____

   f. Why was the chicken sick? It had people pox.

   _____

2. Make up a joke of your own. Write it in the present tense.

   _____

   _____

Verb Tense

A verb can be in the active or the passive voice. The voice of the verb tells whether the subject is doing the action (active voice) or whether something is being done to the subject (passive voice). When the passive voice is used, the verb includes an auxiliary (helping verb) and a participle (main verb).

Active voice: **Katy *read* the book.**

Passive voice: **The book *was read* by Katy.**

1. **Make these sentences more direct by rewriting them in the active voice.**

   a. A big, hairy spider was eaten by my dog.

   _____

   b. The games are chosen by the children.

   _____

   c. The flowers are picked by the gardener.

   _____

   d. Five goals were kicked by Ned.

   _____

   e. The car was crashed by my father.

   _____

   f. The children were snapped at by the injured dog.

   _____

2. **Make these public notices less aggressive by rewriting them in the passive voice.**

   a. Do not put your feet on the seats!

   _____

   b. Keep your dog on a leash!

   _____

   c. Put your trash in the bin!

   _____

   d. We do not allow running!

   _____

Verbs

Verbs can be formed from other parts of speech.

1. **Complete each sentence by making a verb from the word in parentheses.**

   a. The woman _____ that she was innocent. (**proof**)

   b. "I _____ we will arrive soon," said Tim. (**hopefulness**)

   c. You will _____ well if you come with us. (**behavior**)

   d. I did not _____ his incredible story. (**belief**)

   e. The teacher _____ the chalkboard. (**cleanliness**)

   f. We _____ loudly at his jokes. (**laughter**)

2. **Write the present tense (first person) verb form for each of the following words.**

   a. departure _____

   b. enjoyment _____

   c. collection _____

   d. preparation _____

   e. swimmer _____

   f. drawing _____

   g. entrance _____

   h. decoration _____

   i. invitation _____

   j. government _____

3. **Write sentences using the following words as (a.) nouns and (b.) verbs.**

dream	sail	point

   a. noun: _____

   b. verb: _____

   a. noun: _____

   b. verb: _____

   a. noun: _____

   b. verb: _____

Plural Verbs

If the subject of a sentence is plural, the verb should be plural.
If the subject is singular, the verb should be singular.
If there is more than one subject joined by *and*, the verb should be plural.
Collective nouns usually take a singular verb.

1. **Circle the subject. Then choose the correct verb from the parentheses.**

   a. This dog _____ friendly. (is are)

   b. These dogs _____ friendly. (is are)

   c. We _____ going to the zoo. (am are)

   d. I _____ going to the zoo. (am are)

   e. She _____ faster than I do. (runs run)

   f. They _____ faster than I do. (runs run)

2. **Circle the subject. Then choose the correct verb from the parentheses.**

   a. A new pack of cards _____ opened. (was were)

   b. The swarm of bees _____ approaching. (is are)

   c. A school of whales _____ sighted off the coast. (was were)

   d. The party of climbers _____ returned from the mountain. (has have)

   e. The football team _____ tonight. (practices practice)

   f. A sack of potatoes _____ on the road. (is are)

3. **Circle the subject. Then choose the correct verb from the parentheses.**

   a. Mom and Dad _____ on their way. (is are)

   b. Here _____ the bride and groom. (comes come)

   c. Sarah and Zoe _____ going away today. (is are)

   d. The parents and teachers _____ every month. (meets meet)

   e. Jack and Freya _____ very hard. (works work)

   f. Ned and Max _____ to meet me here. (was were)

Adjectives

Introduction

Adjectives are words that tell us more about nouns or pronouns by describing them, adding detail to them, or refining their meaning. By using adjectives, we can add meaning and interest to sentences. Students should also come to understand that a completely different picture can be produced by changing the adjectives in a sentence.

Examples: The *resentful* girl showed the *cranky* lady the way.

The *kind* girl showed the *old* lady the way.

The *savage* dog chased the *frightened* boy.

The *playful* dog chased the *laughing* boy.

Children should be encouraged to think about the adjectives they choose and to steer away from adjectives that have become meaningless through overuse, such as *nice* and *good*.

Examples: It was a *nice* day.   It was a *sunny* day.

It was a *good* story.   It was an *exciting* story.

An adjective can come before or after the noun or pronoun it is describing.

Examples: *The big, black dog came back.*

The dog was big and black.

There are many types of adjectives. Fifth and sixth grade students need to develop an awareness of the following types of adjectives and their uses.

(a) **Describing adjectives** are the most common. They are used to describe, or tell us about the quality of, a noun or pronoun.

Examples: *new   old   beautiful   ugly   big   small*

(b) **Demonstrative adjectives** (sometimes called determiners) are used to point out which noun is being spoken of.

Examples: *That* toy belongs to Katy.

This toy belongs to me.

Those boxes were taken away.

These boxes were left behind.

(c) **Possessive adjectives** are used to show possession.

Examples: This is *my* pen.

Here is *your* hat.

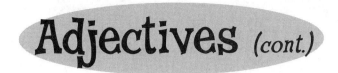

Adjectives (cont.)

The possessive adjectives follow:

	Singular	Plural
First person	my	our
Second person	your	your
Third person	his, her, its	their

(d) **Limiting or number adjectives** indicate number or quantity.

Examples: *two* horses   *ten* fingers
the *first* person in the line   the *second* month

(e) **Indefinite adjectives** are also used to refer to number, but they do not tell us the exact number.

Examples: *Some* boys carried the tent.
Much fuss was made over the new baby.
Few suggestions were received.
Many cars were held up in the traffic jam.

Adjectives can change their form to indicate **degrees of comparison**. The three degrees follow:

* **Positive Degree**—This is the simple form of the adjective.

    Examples: a *sweet* apple   a *muddy* boy   a *beautiful* rose

* **Comparative Degree**—This is used when we compare two people or things. We usually add *-er* to the adjective, but for longer words we sometimes put *more* in front of the adjective.

    Examples: a *sweeter* apple   a *muddier* boy   a *more beautiful* rose

* **Superlative Degree**—This is the highest degree and is used when we compare more than two people or things. It is made by adding *-est* to the adjective or putting *most* in front of the adjective.

    Examples: the *sweetest* apple   the *muddiest* boy   the *most beautiful* rose

Things to remember:

* Some adjectives add *-er* or *-est* without any change to their spelling.
    Examples: *tall*   *taller*   *tallest*

* Adjectives that end in *-e* drop the *-e* when adding *-er* or *-est*.
    Examples: *large*   *larger*   *largest*

Adjectives (cont.)

- If the adjective ends in -*y*, the -*y* is changed to -*i* before adding -*er* or -*est*.

  Examples: *heavy*   *heavier*   *heaviest*

- In some adjectives the last letter is doubled before adding -*er* or -*est*.

  Examples: *big*   *bigger*   *biggest*

- Adjectives of three syllables (and even some of two syllables) have *more* before them for the comparative degree and *most* before them for the superlative degree.

  Examples: *effective*   *more effective*   *most effective*

- Some adjectives have only a simple degree. For example, a thing can only be *dead*; it cannot be more dead.

  Other examples: *full*   *empty*   *straight*   *perfect*   *correct*

To recognize an adjective, ask questions such as these:

What kind of thing?

How many of the thing?

Which thing?

> *The old cars were demolished.*
> What kinds of cars were demolished?   *old* (descriptive adjective)
> *Six flowers were in the glass vase.*
> How many flowers were in the vase?   *six* (number adjective)
> What kind of vase were they in?   *glass* (descriptive adjective)
> *Those girls are going fishing.*
> Which girls are going?   *those* (demonstrative adjective)

Teaching Strategies

Stretch the joke

Write a story, preferably a short joke, on the board. Underline all the nouns. Have children rewrite the story, adding adjectives to the nouns.

Two caterpillars were eating grass in a garden when a butterfly flew overhead.

Two large, fat caterpillars were eating delicious grass …

Self-esteem adjectives

Have children describe each other by using positive adjectives.

Tom is a happy boy.

Ellen is a fast runner.

Adjectives *(cont.)*

Missing nouns

Give children a list of adjectives and have them add suitable nouns.

curly _____   *delicious* _____

black _____   *sharp* _____

three _____   *savage* _____

For sale

Have children add suitable adjectives to mock advertisements.

FOR SALE: HOUSE, ROOF, ROOMS, GARAGE, ETC.

FOR SALE: LARGE HOUSE, TILE ROOF, EIGHT ROOMS, TWO-CAR GARAGE, ETC.

Opposites quiz

Read out a list of adjectives. Have children call out or write the opposites. This can be played in teams. The first team to score ten is the winning team.

stopping/starting   *right/wrong*   *careless/careful*

useful/useless   *straight/bent*

Portraits

Have children cut out a picture of a person (possibly someone well-known) from a magazine. Have them write sentences which include appropriate adjectives.

This lady has black hair.

She is leading two dogs.

Adjective mix-up

Divide the class into two groups. Ask one group to make a list of nouns. Ask the other group to make a list of adjectives. Now have the children try to fit each adjective beside a noun it could describe.

adjective list   noun list

empty   *classroom*

crowded   *grass*

tall   *bucket*

Newspaper hunt

Have children read through newspapers and magazines and cut out any interesting adjectives they find. Make a large class adjective chart. Encourage children to refer to the chart when they need an adjective for their own writing.

WORD BANK

Adjectives

Descriptive Adjectives

amazing	dry	immense	scarlet
bright	elegant	narrow	secluded
deserted	enormous	naughty	violet
desolate	gorgeous	occasional	yellow
disgusting	gruesome	rich	young

Demonstrative Adjectives	Possessive Adjectives	Number Adjectives	Indefinite Adjectives
such	her	hundred	all
that	my	two	few
these	our	fifth	many
this	their	hundredth	several
those	your	second	some

Proper Adjectives	Positive Adjectives	Comparative Adjectives	Superlative Adjectives
Siberian	good	better	best
English	little	less	least
Venetian	many	more	most
Indian	much	more	most
Brazilian	bad	worse	worst

Adjectives Not Compared | ## More Descriptive Adjectives

Adjectives Not Compared	More Descriptive Adjectives		
perfect	accidental	melodious	skillful
unique	beautiful	nonsensical	squalid
square	crafty	ornamental	starry
universal	disastrous	perilous	sunny
wrong	effective	picturesque	sympathetic
fatal	faithful	querulous	tempestuous
full	graceful	quaint	tribal
mortal	heroic	responsive	victorious
supreme	injurious	scholastic	vigorous
blind	luxurious	sensible	wretched

Adjectives

Describing adjectives are used to describe a noun or pronoun.

1. Choose a word from the box to complete each sentence.

> circular   fragile   broad   careful   perilous   childish

a. A river that is wide is _____ .

b. Something easily broken is _____ .

c. If something is round, it is _____ .

d. An immature person is _____ .

e. If something is dangerous, it is _____ .

f. If a person is cautious, he or she is _____ .

2. Choose the most suitable describing adjective from the box.

> delicious   rusty   sunny   savage   interesting   woolen   ripe   clever

a. _____ story   e. _____ sweater

b. _____ student   f. _____ weather

c. _____ knife   g. _____ apple

d. _____ food   h. _____ watchdog

3. Rewrite the story, replacing each underlined adjective with one of a similar meaning from the box.

> big   minute   scared   thick   strong   high   sour   fat

As we walked through the <u>dense</u> forest, we saw a <u>plump</u> bird eating some <u>bitter</u> fruit that grew on a <u>tall</u> tree. My brother Sam, a <u>sturdy</u> lad, threw a <u>tiny</u> pebble at the bird. The <u>frightened</u> bird flew to the safety of a <u>gigantic</u> bush.

_____

_____

_____

_____

Adjectives

Describing adjectives are used to describe a noun or pronoun.

1. **Choose from the box the describing adjective that has the opposite meaning to the adjective in the parentheses.**

> plump   foolish   dangerous   false   fresh   deep

   a. This loaf of bread is _____ . (**stale**)

   b. This is a _____ spot to swim. (**safe**)

   c. The pool is very _____ here. (**shallow**)

   d. I knew his statement was _____ . (**true**)

   e. This pig is quite _____ . (**thin**)

   f. Tom is a _____ boy. (**wise**)

2. **Choose from the box the describing adjective that has a similar meaning to the adjective in the parentheses.**

> careful   sudden   peculiar   serious   sharp   sacred

   a. I found her to be a _____ person. (**odd**)

   b. Paul is a very _____ boy. (**cautious**)

   c. We were startled by the _____ movement. (**abrupt**)

   d. It was a _____ breach of the rules. (**grave**)

   e. She felt a _____ pain in her arm. (**acute**)

   f. We entered the _____ temple quietly. (**holy**)

3. **If the adjectives have a similar meaning, write S. If they have an opposite meaning, write O.**

   a. plentiful   abundant _____   e. cordial   friendly   _____

   b. dreary   exciting _____   f. feeble   strong   _____

   c. soft   tender _____   g. awkward   graceful   _____

   d. private   public _____   h. drowsy   sleepy   _____

Adjectives

Name _____   Grammar BLM **25**

Number adjectives are used to show the number of things or the numerical order of things.

Indefinite adjectives are also used to refer to number, but they do not tell us the exact number.

1. **Choose from the box an adjective to complete each sentence.**

> twelve   three   two   ten   eight   four   fourteen   one hundred

- a. There are _____ eggs in a dozen.
- b. A bicycle has _____ wheels.
- c. There are _____ years in a decade.
- d. A tricycle has _____ wheels.
- e. A century is _____ years.
- f. There are _____ days in a fortnight.
- g. A square has _____ sides.
- h. An octopus has _____ tentacles.

2. **Choose the number adjective from the parentheses to complete each sentence.**

- a. February is the _____ month. (**second hottest**)
- b. I am the _____ person in the line. (**first shortest**)
- c. Did you see the _____ cyclist? (**hairy fourth**)
- d. I would like the _____ book on that shelf, please. (**fifth fat**)
- e. Katy lives in the _____ house on Avenue Road. (**white third**)
- f. The _____ swimmer stood on the blocks. (**cold sixth**)

3. **Write sentences using the following as indefinite adjectives.**

> some   few   many   most   much

- a. _____
- b. _____
- c. _____
- d. _____
- e. _____

Adjectives

Demonstrative adjectives are used to point out which noun is being spoken of.

That **toy belongs to Katy.**

This **toy belongs to me.**

1. **Choose from the box a demonstrative adjective to complete each sentence. Then circle the noun that the adjective points out.**

those	these	this	such	that

   a. _____ shoes are made of crocodile skin.

   b. What are you going to do with _____ tables?

   c. _____ cow had twin calves.

   d. _____ day has been the worst day of my life.

   e. _____ silliness is to be discouraged.

2. **Now use the demonstrative adjectives in sentences of your own. In each sentence underline the adjective and circle the noun it points out.**

   a. _____

   b. _____

   c. _____

   d. _____

   e. _____

Possessive adjectives are used to show ownership.

This is *my* **pen.**

Here is *your* **hat.**

3. **Underline the possessive adjectives.**

   a. My dog is very funny. He bites his tail as he runs around.

   b. Your pencils are on the table next to our books.

   c. Their cat is licking its paws.

   d. Her bedroom is untidy, but your bedroom is neat.

Adjectives

Adjectives can be formed from words also used as other parts of speech.

1. **Complete each sentence by forming an adjective from the word in parentheses.**

   a. I fell asleep in the _____ chair. (**comfort**)

   b. The _____ animal was captured by the park rangers. (**danger**)

   c. It was a _____ day when the children left. (**storm**)

   d. Mr. Smith is a very _____ person. (**patience**)

   e. This is an extremely _____ painting. (**value**)

   f. The _____ film star visited our town recently. (**fame**)

2. **Form an adjective from each word.**

   a. anger _____ parent   e. coward _____ act

   b. child _____ act   f. favor _____ food

   c. friend _____ person   g. fur _____ rabbit

   d. expense _____ perfume   h. haste _____ decision

3. **Write sentences of your own, using adjectives formed from the following words.**

   | a. noise   b. water   c. luxury   d. sense   e. mercy   f. nation |

   a. _____

   b. _____

   c. _____

   d. _____

   e. _____

   f. _____

Adjectives

Proper adjectives are formed from proper nouns. Proper adjectives also begin with a capital letter.

1. **Write the proper adjective formed from the proper noun in parentheses.**

   a. I ate some _____ food. (**China**)

   b. The guide showed us around the _____ village. (**Wales**)

   c. Is this a _____ watch? (**Switzerland**)

   d. The _____ flag is blue and white. (**Greece**)

   e. My mother's friend speaks with a _____ accent. (**Scotland**)

   f. My uncle bought a bottle of _____ wine. (**France**)

2. **Write the proper adjective formed from the proper noun.**

   a. Turkey _____   e. Mexico _____

   b. Sweden _____   f. Japan _____

   c. Britain _____   g. Italy _____

   d. Tibet _____   h. Egypt _____

3. **The following athletes represent their countries. Underline the proper adjective and write the proper noun on the line.**

   a. A Turkish runner won the marathon. _____

   b. A Dutch weightlifter won the gold medal. _____

   c. An Irish athlete won the 200m hurdle. _____

   d. A Norwegian swimmer won in the distance event. _____

   e. A Spanish team won the rowing event. _____

   f. A Brazilian boxer won the lightweight contest. _____

Adjectives

Adjectives can change their form to show degrees of comparison.

Positive Degree	Comparative Degree	Superlative Degree
sweet	sweeter	sweetest
muddy	muddier	muddiest
beautiful	more beautiful	most beautiful

1. **Complete these sentences by writing the correct degree of the adjective in parentheses.**

   a. This is the _____ building in the city. (**old**)

   b. My puppy is _____ than your puppy. (**young**)

   c. My brother is _____ than I am. (**short**)

   d. Today is _____ than yesterday. (**cold**)

   e. Katy bought the _____ toy in the shop. (**cute**)

   f. Tim's mouse was the _____ of all the pets. (**small**)

2. **Complete the table.**

Positive degree	Comparative degree	Superlative degree
safe	safer	
wise		
pale		
		bravest
	larger	

3. **Complete these sentences by writing the correct degree of the adjective in parentheses. Hint: If the adjective has a short vowel and ends with a single consonant, the last letter is doubled before adding -er or -est.**

   a. These are the _____ apples in the supermarket. (**big**)

   b. This pig is much _____ than that pig. (**fat**)

   c. That story was the _____ I've ever heard. (**sad**)

   d. Today was the _____ day we've had for ten years. (**hot**)

Adjectives

Adjectives can change their form to show degrees of comparison.

Positive Degree	Comparative Degree	Superlative Degree
sweet	sweeter	sweetest
muddy	muddier	muddiest
beautiful	more beautiful	most beautiful

1. **Complete these sentences by writing the correct degree of the adjective in parentheses. Hint: If the adjective ends in -y, change the -y to -i before adding -er or -est.**

   a. Mike must be the _____ boy in the whole school. (busy)

   b. This box is much _____ than that one. (heavy)

   c. You always seem to be _____ than I am. (lucky)

   d. This kitten is the _____ of the whole litter. (noisy)

2. **Circle the correct adjective. Hint: Some adjectives have irregular forms.**

   a. He is (gooder better) than I am at marbles.

   b. This is the (worst baddest) day I've had all year.

   c. Joanne has (less fewer) cherries than I have.

   d. Tom is the (morest most) reliable boy in the class.

3. **Complete the chart. Hint: Adjectives of three syllables, and some of two syllables, have more written before them for the comparative degree and most for the superlative degree.**

Positive Degree	Comparative Degree	Superlative Degree
beautiful		
	more luxurious	
efficient		
	more humorous	
		most delicious
sorrowful		
		most comfortable

©Teacher Created Resources, Inc.

Adverbs

Introduction

An **adverb** is a word that adds meaning to a verb, an adjective, or another adverb. There are many types of adverbs. The most important types for students to recognize are the following:

(a) **Adverbs of Place**—These are used to show where something happens.
I told him to come *here*.
Other examples: *above   below   upstairs   outside   everywhere*

(b) **Adverbs of Time**—These are used to show when something happens.
He played *yesterday*.
Other examples: *soon   later   yesterday   today   often*
seldom   never   already   now   then

(c) **Adverbs of Manner**—These are used to show how something happens.
The child cried *loudly*.
Other examples: *quietly   furiously   helplessly   softly   gently   noisily*

(d) **Interrogative Adverbs**—These ask questions.
How are you?
Other examples: *when   where   why   how   who*

(e) **Affirmative, Negative, or Modal Adverbs**—These adverbs express the negative, agreement, or doubt.
He is *not* coming.
Other examples: *never   no   perhaps   possibly   probably   yes*

Like adjectives, adverbs can change their form to indicate degrees of comparison. The three degrees are these:

• **Positive Degree**—This refers to one person or thing.
Example: Tom can play *hard*.

• **Comparative Degree**—This compares two people or things.
Example: Tom can play *harder*.

• **Superlative Degree**—This compares more than two people or things.
Example: Of the three children, Tom plays *hardest*.

Things to remember:

• To adverbs of one syllable, add *-er* and *-est* to form the comparative and superlative.
Examples: *hard   harder   hardest*

• Adverbs that end in *-ly* have *more* and *most* placed before them to form the comparative and superlative.
Examples: *loudly   more loudly   most loudly*

Adverbs (cont.)

- Some adverbs are irregular and must be learned individually.
  Examples:

badly	*worse*	*worst*
well	*better*	*best*
much	*more*	*most*

- Some adverbs look like adjectives. You can tell they are adverbs if they add meaning to verbs, adjectives, and other adverbs. If a word adds meaning to a noun or pronoun, it is an adjective.

Teaching Strategies

Give me one
Have children provide one word to replace a group of words in a sentence that is written on the chalkboard.
Mike always drives in a fast way.
Mike always drives quickly.

How, when, or where?
Have children add words to a sentence written on the chalkboard. The words should tell how, when, or where the action happened.
Mike's bike was stolen . . . (when)   yesterday.
The teacher told me to put it over . . . (where)   there.
Billy did her work . . . (how)   neatly.

Adverb list
Have children list suitable adverbs to complete a sentence.
I can walk . . .
quickly   slowly   rapidly   proudly   lazily   awkwardly
Other suitable verbs to use for this exercise include swim, speak, creep, sleep, fight, wait, eat, laugh, dance, read, etc.

Similar or opposite?
Call out an adverb or write an adverb on the chalkboard. Have children provide an adverb of similar meaning or one of opposite meaning.
rapidly: quickly   slowly
loudly: noisily   softly

Act the adverb
Have children carry out a number of actions in different manners.
walk: quickly   carefully   foolishly

WORD BANK

Adverbs

Adverbs of Place

above
behind
below
downstairs
elsewhere
everywhere
here
inside
near
nowhere
outside
somewhere
upstairs
within
yonder

Adverbs of Time

already
immediately
instantly
late
lately
meanwhile
never
now
often
presently
recently
seldom
shortly
soon
then
today
yesterday
yet

Adverbs of Manner

anxiously
carefully
desperately
furiously
helpfully
ill
jauntily
loudly
nervously
noisily
powerfully
quietly
rapidly
skillfully
so
tearfully
trustingly
urgently
vigorously
well

Interrogative Adverbs

how
when
whence
where
whither
why

Affirmative, Negative, or Modal Adverbs

never
no
not
not at all
perhaps
possibly
probably

Adverbs

An adverb is a word that adds meaning to a verb, an adjective, or another adverb.

1. **Select the best adverb to complete each sentence.**

gracefully	neatly	busily	angrily
brightly	tightly	softly	carefully

   a. We should cross a busy street _____ .

   b. We tie parcels _____ .

   c. Lights can shine _____ .

   d. We should write _____ in our books.

   e. The children worked _____ .

   f. The lion roared _____ .

   g. We should whisper _____ .

   h. A swan swims _____ .

2. **Beside each adverb write *how*, *when*, or   to show what it tells us.**

   a. tomorrow _____   f. yesterday _____

   b. greedily _____   g. inside _____

   c. tonight _____   h. down _____

   d. today _____   i. sweetly _____

   e. sadly _____   j. outside _____

3. **Add an adverb of your own to complete each sentence. Make sure your adverb answers the word in parentheses.**

   a. She fell _____ . (**where**)

   b. He whistled _____ . (**how**)

   c. Tom arrived _____ . (**when**)

   d. The window was broken _____ . (**how**)

   e. The kangaroo jumped the fence _____ . (**how**)

   f. I will repay you _____ . (**when**)

Adverbs

An adverb is a word that adds meaning to a verb, an adjective, or another adverb.

1. **Select the best adverb that tells *where* to complete each sentence.**

out	everywhere	there	here
nowhere	below	somewhere	inside

   a. Put the boxes over _____ .

   b. The lost pens were _____ to be found.

   c. I can't find it, but I must have put it _____ .

   d. Let's sit right _____ .

   e. They stayed on the top deck, but I went _____ .

   f. When she dropped the bottle, the water spilled _____ .

   g. He was so angry he stormed _____ .

   h. Tim went outside, but I stayed _____ .

2. **Add an adverb that tells *how* to each verb.**

politely	swiftly	softly	loudly
heavily	happily	slowly	sweetly

   a. fell _____   e. yelled _____

   b. whispered _____   f. limped _____

   c. sang _____   g. spoke _____

   d. ran _____   h. played _____

3. **To each pair of sentences add an adverb that tells *where* and then an adverb that tells *how*.**

   a. Ben played _____ .   Ben played _____ .

   b. I told her to come _____ .   I told her to come _____ .

   c. The fish swam _____ .   The fish swam _____ .

Adverbs

An adverb is a word that adds meaning to a verb, an adjective, or another adverb.

1. **Write an adverb to replace the words in parentheses.**

   a. The old man was sleeping (**in peace**).   _____

   b. Our teacher left the room (**in a hurry**).   _____

   c. Lisa jumped the fence (**with ease**).   _____

   d. We are going to leave (**in a short time**).   _____

   e. Tim arrived (**after the expected time**).   _____

   f. He gazed (**with pride**) at his good writing.   _____

2. **Add an adverb from the box to complete each sentence.**

wearily	here	upstairs	now
tomorrow	tonight	punctually	noisily

   a. We must leave right _____.

   b. Put it _____ .

   c. Paul arrived _____.

   d. Ben yawned _____.

   e. The stars are shining brightly _____.

   f. The match will be played _____.

   g. There was a party _____.

   h. The monkeys chattered _____.

3. **Add an adverb of your own to complete each sentence.**

   a. The children wandered _____ .

   b. Sally always speaks _____.

   c. I cuddled the baby rabbit _____.

   d. Mike crossed the busy road _____.

   e. The man fell _____.

Adverbs

An adverb is a word that adds meaning to a verb, an adjective, or another adverb.

1. **Write the adverb that has a similar meaning.**

tidily	feebly	glumly	foolishly
abruptly	gently	gladly	rapidly

a. weakly _____

b. happily _____

c. neatly _____

d. stupidly _____

e. softly _____

f. sadly _____

g. suddenly _____

h. quickly _____

2. **Write the adverb that has the opposite meaning.**

swiftly	angrily	politely	neatly
bravely	suddenly	later	yesterday

a. untidily _____

b. slowly _____

c. happily _____

d. cowardly _____

e. rudely _____

f. tomorrow _____

g. gradually _____

h. immediately _____

3. **If the adverbs have a similar meaning, write S. If they have the opposite meaning, write O.**

a. always   never   _____

b. angrily   furiously   _____

c. there   nowhere   _____

d. never   always   _____

e. lazily   idly   _____

f. carefully   carelessly   _____

g. gracefully   awkwardly   _____

h. distinctly   clearly   _____

Adverbs

Adverbs can be formed from other parts of speech.

1. Complete each sentence by forming an adverb from the word in parentheses.

   a. The girl sang _____ . (sweet)

   b. We waited _____ . (patient)

   c. Sam ran _____ . (quick)

   d. The crash happened _____ . (sudden)

   e. She accepted the food _____ . (glad)

   f. Sam is feeling _____ . (poor)

2. Complete each sentence by forming an adverb from the word in parentheses. Hint: If the word ends in -y, change the -y to -i before adding -ly.

   a. We did the work _____ . (easy)

   b. The dog ate the food _____ . (greedy)

   c. He is dressed _____ . (shabby)

   d. She fell _____ . (clumsy)

   e. He walked_____around the house. (lazy)

   f. They sang the song _____ . (merry)

3. Complete each sentence by forming an adverb from a word in the box. Hint: If the word ends in -e, drop the -e before adding -ly to make the adverb.

humble	idle	feeble	gentle	comfortable

   a. He held the baby _____ .

   b. She sat _____ in the chair.

   c. He accepted the prize _____ .

   d. The boy lazed _____ .

   e. The ill man walked _____ .

Articles

Introduction

There are three **articles**: *the, a,* and *an*. Articles can be either **definite** or **indefinite**. Fifth and sixth grade students should be able to identify definite and indefinite articles.

(a) *The* is the **definite article**. It is definite because it is referring to a specific thing.

Examples: *The* man lives next door.   *The* dog is outside.

(b) *A* and *an* are **indefinite**. Rather than referring to any specific thing, they refer to any one of a group of things.

Examples: *A* man lives next door.   *A* dog is outside.

An is used instead of *a* in front of words that begin with a vowel (a, e, i, o, u).
An is also used in front of words that begin with a silent *h*.

Examples: *an* apple *an* egg *an* igloo *an* orange *an* umbrella
        an hour but *a* hotel

Teaching Strategies

The missing article
Allow children to develop their own paragraphs or short stories, leaving out the articles—*the, a,* and *an*. They can then give the puzzles to their classmates to solve.

Make it definite
Have children change an indefinite article to the definite article, adding descriptive words to help.

I saw a dog.

I saw the big, black dog.

A or an?
Provide lists of words. Have children add *a* or *an* to introduce each.

_____ *box* _____ *egg*

Articles

Use *an* instead of *a* in front of words that begin with a vowel.

1. Write *a* or *an* in the spaces.

   a. One day _____ man saw _____ monkey climbing _____ tall tree

     in _____ dense jungle.

   b. Mike ate _____ orange and _____ apple for his lunch. Sometime later he

     ate _____ pie.

   c. _____ athlete must train hard if she is to win _____ race.

   d. On our farm there are lots of hens. One hen laid _____ egg on _____

     branch of _____ tall tree.

   e. Sue has _____ aunt who lives in Las Vegas and _____ uncle who

     lives in Reno.

2. Write *a* or *an* in the spaces.

   a. _____ orange

   b. _____ underarm pitch

   c. _____ dozen eggs

   d. _____ big shed

   e. _____ ocean liner

   f. _____ book

   g. _____ endangered species

   h. _____ effective cure

   i. _____ paper envelope

   j. _____ obvious mistake

Articles

When we are talking about a particular thing, we use *the*. This is called the definite article.

When we are talking about a general thing, we use *a* or *an*. This is called the indefinite article.

Add *the*, *an*, or *a* in the spaces.

a. One day _____ old man was walking along _____ street. _____ man was wearing _____ orange shirt, and _____ tie he was wearing had black and gold stripes. _____ lady who saw him in _____ supermarket was amused. _____ lady began to laugh at him. _____ old man said she was _____ rude person, and he told her that he was going to _____ fancy-dress ball.

b. Would you like to see _____ new car in the garage? It is _____ only car in this area that has _____ oil cleaning device that cleans _____ engine at all times. _____ uncle of mine had _____ car like it, and he said it was _____ excellent device and _____ asset to all new cars.

c. Would you like _____ pink guinea pig? I have one. It is _____ only pink guinea pig in _____ world. I bought it from _____ old lady I met at _____ pet shop. She said she also had _____ blue rabbit and _____ ostrich that had red and white stripes. She said _____ ostrich was _____ obstinate bird and laid _____ egg every day.

Articles

When we are talking about a particular thing, we use *the*. This is called the definite article.

When we are talking about a general thing, we use *a* or *an*. This is called the indefinite article.

1. **Complete these sentences in your own words. You must include the article in parentheses.**

    a. (the)   A horse galloped _____ .

    b. (an)   I picked _____ .

    c. (a)   I saw _____ .

    d. (the)   Did you see _____ ?

    e. (an)   In the jungle I saw _____ .

    f. (a)   The boys found _____ .

2. **Write *a* or *an* in the spaces.**

    a. There is _____ apple tree, _____ orange tree, _____ banana tree, and _____ lemon tree in our garden.

    b. I picked _____ onion, _____ cabbage, _____ radish, and _____ eggplant from our garden.

    c. On the merry-go-round there is _____ zebra, _____ elephant, _____ ape, and _____ giraffe.

    d. Some birds we saw were _____ ostrich, _____ emu, _____ robin, and _____ eagle.

    e. There is _____ oak tree, _____ elm tree, _____ maple tree, and _____ ash tree growing in the forest.

    f. In the game the children had to point to _____ ear, _____ foot, _____ ankle, and _____ nose.

Articles

When we are talking about a particular thing, we use *the*. This is called the definite article.

When we are talking about a general thing, we use *a* or *an*. This is called the indefinite article.

1. Add *a* or *an* in the spaces.

a. _____ novel excuse   f. _____ incompetent person

b. _____ octagon   g. _____ nugget of gold

c. _____ mysterious event   h. _____ offensive odor

d. _____ official complaint   i. _____ audible sound

e. _____ instant   j. _____ angry cat

2. Add *a*, *an* or *the* in the spaces.

a. _____ company hired _____ assistant to help at _____ auction that
   was being held at _____ salesroom in _____ small country town.
   _____ assistant did not like _____ attitude of _____ manager of
   _____ company, so he left immediately. Everyone thought this was
   _____ awful thing to do as it was very close to _____ day of _____ sale.

b. My mother is _____ expert cook. She cooked _____ enormous cake
   last year and won _____ prize at _____ show. After she had added
   _____ flour to _____ bowl, she cracked _____ egg. She dropped
   _____ egg into _____ bowl and mixed it in. She put _____ cake
   in _____ oven to cook for forty minutes. When it had cooled she put
   it on _____ plate and cut it with _____ sharp knife.

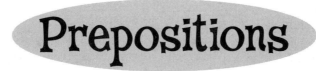

Prepositions

Introduction

Prepositions are words we use to show the relationship of a noun or a pronoun to another word in the sentence. They can be called **place words** because they often tell us the positions of things.

Examples: The puppy is *on* the chair.

The girl is *beside* the chair.

The bone is *under* the chair.

The prepositions *on, beside,* and *under* all refer to the noun *chair.* They tell us the relationship between it and the puppy, the girl, and the bone.

Problem prepositions

among/between

Something is shared *among* several people or things (three or more). Something is shared *between* two people or things.

Examples: *I divided the cake among the whole class.*

I divided the cake between Mary and me.

in/into

In shows position in one place. *Into* shows movement from one place to another.

Examples: *The teacher is in the room.*

The boy dived into the river.

different from

One thing or person is *different from* another. Never say *different than.*

beside/besides

Beside means at the side of. *Besides* means in addition to.

Examples: *The teacher stood beside the table.*

Several girls were there besides Margaret.

Preposition or adverb?

Some prepositions may look like adverbs. To tell whether the word is a preposition or an adverb, look at the way it is used. Look at the following sentences.

I fell down. *Down* is an adverb of place. It tells where I fell.

I walked down the road. *Down* is a preposition governing road.

Remember also that a preposition has a noun or pronoun after it.

Prepositions *(cont.)*

Teaching Strategies

Question time

Ask children to describe the positions of some objects in the classroom. Tell children they must reply using a preposition in a sentence.

Where is the clock?   *The clock is under the picture.*
Where is the television?   *The television is beside the table.*

Preposition opposites

Have children provide the opposites of given prepositions.

The snake crawled over the rock.
The snake crawled under the rock.

Jumbled prepositions

Give children exercises in which the prepositions are jumbled. Have children identify the preposition or write it correctly.

The bird flew (voer) the tree.
The bird flew over the tree.

WORD BANK   Prepositions

above	by	opposite
across	down	outside
after	during	over
against	except	past
among	for	since
around	from	through
at	in	to
before	inside	towards
behind	into	underneath
below	near	until
beside	of	upon
between	off	within
beyond	onto	without

Prepositions

Name _____   Grammar BLM **40**

Prepositions show the relationship of a noun or a pronoun to another word in the sentence. The noun or pronoun follows the preposition and may have modifiers.

1. **Complete each sentence by adding a preposition from the box.**

at	between	from	with	under	down

   a. A line of cars stretched _____ the freeway to the shopping center.

   b. The candies were divided _____ Mary and Sally.

   c. The dog growled _____ the two strangers.

   d. I told her not to interfere _____ the new bicycle.

   e. The snake slithered _____ the rock.

   f. Jack and Jill tripped and rolled _____ the hill.

2. **Unjumble the prepositions.**

   a. Mike is standing _____ Pete. (**ebsdei**)

   b. The cat is _____ the tree. (**enar**)

   c. It is leaning _____ the fence. (**gaainst**)

   d. They ran _____ the garden. (**raound**)

   e. The ball is _____ the table. (**duner**)

   f. The children ran _____ the playground. (**rthough**)

3. **Write the missing preposition.**

   a. I disagree _____ him.

   b. This is similar _____ that.

   c. I have to rely _____ you.

   d. He was found guilty _____ treason.

   e. She was satisfied _____ the agreement.

Prepositions

Prepositions show the relationship of a noun or a pronoun to another word in the sentence. The noun or pronoun follows the preposition.

1. **Circle the correct preposition in the parentheses.**

   a. The key was found still (into beside in) the lock.

   b. The box of books was (of towards on) the table.

   c. The frightened horse galloped (across since among) the field.

   d. She slipped and fell (up down through) the well.

   e. Mike leaned the shovel (below from against) the wall.

   f. I picked the apples (of during off) the tree.

2. **Add different prepositions to give each sentence in the pair a different meaning.**

   a. The vase was _____ the table.

      The vase was _____ the table.

   b. The children ran _____ the tree.

      The children ran _____ the tree.

   c. The jet landed _____ the airport.

      The jet landed _____ the airport.

3. **Write sentences of your own, using prepositions from the box.**

against	over	under	between	off	below	near	down

   a. _____

   b. _____

   c. _____

   d. _____

   e. _____

   f. _____

Prepositions

Name _____ Grammar BLM **42**

Prepositions show the relationship of a noun or a pronoun to another word in the sentence. The noun or pronoun follows the preposition and is the object of the prepostion. It may have modifiers.

1. **In each sentence circle the preposition and underline the object of the preposition.**

   a. We played in the park.

   b. We went to the farm.

   c. I looked underneath the table.

   d. I sat on the lawn.

   e. Tom went through the trees.

2. **Circle the prepositions in the grid and then use them to fill the spaces in the sentences.**

t	h	r	o	u	g	h
o	f	p	d	w	o	i
v	r	a	o	i	f	n
e	o	s	w	t	f	t
r	m	t	n	h	x	o

   a. The kangaroo jumped _____ the fence.

   b. He dived from the board _____ the water.

   c. I walked _____ my old school again.

   d. I walked _____ the thick grass.

   e. The lamp was knocked _____ the table.

   f. Your bike is different _____ mine.

   g. Mike slipped and fell _____ the hole.

   h. Do not interfere _____ the new workers.

Pronouns

Introduction

Fifth and sixth grade students should understand that we use **pronouns** to take the place of **nouns**. By using pronouns we can talk about people or things without naming them. This helps keep our use of language from becoming disjointed because of too much repetition.

Without pronouns we would have to write like this:

> *Bill said that Bill could not come because Bill's father had not bought Bill a new pair of sneakers.*

Children can quickly see the need for pronouns when they read this.

There are many types of pronouns. Those appropriate for fifth and sixth graders to learn are these:

(a) **Personal pronouns**—Here are the personal pronouns that students should be familiar with and be able to use without difficulty.

	Nominative		Objective	
	Singular	**Plural**	**Singular**	**Plural**
First person	I	we	me	us
Second person	you	you	you	you
Third person	he, she, it	they	him, her, it	them

Things to remember:

* If a pronoun is the **subject** or part of the subject of a sentence, it is in the **nominative** case.

  Example: *She* is coming to my house.

  If a pronoun is the **object** or **indirect object** in a sentence, it is in the **objective** case.

  Example: I gave *her* the book.

* **First person** pronouns are used if we are talking about ourselves.
  Examples: *I* am nine years old.
  We are learning about sharks.

  Second person pronouns are used if we are talking to someone.
  Example: Are *you* going to be long?

Pronouns *(cont.)*

Third person pronouns are used if we are talking about someone or something else.

Examples: *She* was late for school.
              They arrived by bus.
              It was on the table.

(b) **Possessive pronouns**—Students should also be familiar with the following possessive pronouns.

	Singular	**Plural**
First person	mine	ours
Second person	yours	yours
Third person	his, hers, its	theirs

Remember, possessive pronouns can function as possessive adjectives. Look at the following sentence.

His book is here. *His* is a possessive adjective describing *book*.

For more information about possessive adjectives, see the section on adjectives.

(c) **Relative pronouns**—These not only take the place of nouns but also help join sentences. The relative pronouns are the following:

    who   *whom*   *which*   *that*

Who and *whom* are used to refer to people. *Who* is the nominative case and is used when referring to the subject of the verb. *Whom* is the objective case and is used when referring to the object of the verb.

Examples: The girl *who* wore the blue hat is my sister.
              The friend with *whom* I went to the park lost his wallet.

Which and *that* are used to refer to animals, places, and things.

(d) **Interrogative pronouns**—These pronouns ask questions.

Examples: *Who* paid?
              What is that?

Other interrogative pronouns are *whom, whose, which.*
However, if the word is followed by a noun, it is not an interrogative pronoun. It is an interrogative adjective.

(e) **Demonstrative pronouns**—These are pronouns that stand for and point out nouns.

Example: *This* is the train for Sydney.

Other demonstrative pronouns are *that, those, these*.

Pronouns *(cont.)*

However, if the word is followed by a noun, it is not a demonstrative pronoun. It is a demonstrative adjective.

(f) **Indefinite pronouns**—These pronouns stand for a person, place, or thing which is not particularly defined. They usually take a singular verb.

Example: Is *anyone* interested in football?

Other indefinite pronouns are these:

one	*none*	*somebody*	*everyone*	*someone*
anybody	*anything*	*no one*	*nobody*	*everything*

Problem pronouns

its/it's

Its is a pronoun that means "belonging to it." *It's* is not a pronoun. It is a contraction of *it is*.

I/me

Sometimes it is difficult to decide when to use *I* or *me* in a sentence. If in doubt, divide the sentence into two short sentences.

> *Mike is going to the circus.*
> *I am going to the circus.*
> So the correct usage is *Mike and I are going to the circus.*
> *Jack told Sally to get off the grass.*
> *Jack told me to get off the grass.*
> So the correct usage is *Jack told Sally and me to get off the grass.*

Teaching Strategies

Pronoun cloze

Write a passage on the chalkboard, leaving spaces for the pronouns. Write the missing pronouns on small pieces of cardboard and have children work in groups to stick them in the correct spaces.

Jane carried the glass to the kitchen. At the sink _____ dropped _____.

Pronoun search

Conduct a pronoun search from a common text, such as a photocopy of a story or poem already read. Have children read the text and circle any pronouns they find.

Buzz!

Read a short passage aloud. Tell children that when they hear a pronoun, they must shout out "Buzz!" (You might want to practice with one sentence.) Points can be awarded for correctly identifying the pronouns.

Pronouns

Name _____

Pronouns are words that take the places of nouns.

1. **Rewrite each sentence, replacing the underlined words with a pronoun.**

    a. The lady said that <u>the lady</u> was leaving now.

    _____

    b. When the dog stopped barking, it went back to <u>the dog's</u> kennel.

    _____

    c. The teacher told them that <u>the teacher</u> wanted them to work harder.

    _____

    d. The puppies whimpered when <u>the puppies</u> were hungry.

    _____

    e. The queen dismissed <u>the queen's</u> servants.

    _____

    f. Tom's father asked <u>Tom</u> to cut the wood.

    _____

2. **Color the boxes that contain a pronoun.**

we	paper	us	he
their	they	you	window
rabbit	jealous	my	mine
them	quickly	she	shiny
table	yours	over	silver

Pronouns

Name _____   Grammar BLM **44**

Pronouns are words that take the places of nouns.

1. Add a possessive pronoun to complete each sentence.

> yours   theirs   hers   his   mine   ours   its

   a. This dog belongs to him. This dog is _____ .

   b. This book belongs to Sally. This book is _____ .

   c. This cup belongs to me. This cup is _____ .

   d. We must take responsibility. The responsibility is _____ .

   e. The horses belong to them. The horses are _____ .

   f. This pen belongs to you. This pen is _____ .

   g. This collar belongs to the dog. This collar is _____ .

2. Use the pronouns in the box to complete the story.

> he   she   her   they   it   him   mine   their

Last Tuesday the boys decided _____ would go fishing. They put all

_____ gear in the trunk of the car. Mary was angry because the boys

had put _____ rod in the car. It made her feel upset because

_____ had only got the rod last week. She told her father, and

_____ agreed with her and asked the boys to put _____

back in the shed. Sam protested. "It is _____ !" he said. Mary began to

cry. "I will not let _____ have it!" she sobbed.

3. Circle the noun that the underlined pronoun refers to.

   a. Lisa called the puppy to the kitchen so <u>she</u> could wash it.

   b. Jack and Jill went up the hill, but <u>he</u> slipped and fell down.

   c. My father bought some candies. He gave <u>them</u> to me.

   d. These flowers are from my little sister. <u>She</u> picked them for you.

Pronouns

Name _____   Grammar BLM **45**

Pronouns are words that take the places of nouns.

1. Use a possessive pronoun from the box to complete each sentence.

their	his	our	my	ours	its	mine	her

a. I rode _____ bike to the soccer match.

b. Sally looked after _____ dogs while we were away.

c. I can't see Billy. Is that _____ bike there?

d. Mr. and Mrs. Smith have arrived. _____ car is in the driveway.

e. Sally left _____ backpack in the classroom.

f. Don't touch these pencils. They are _____.

g. The dog hurt _____ leg when it was run over.

h. They grow carrots too, but _____ are much better.

2. Circle the correct word in the parentheses.

a. (My Me) friend said he would see (you your) later.

b. That house is (our ours). Which house is (your yours)?

c. Sally said this is (hers her). Does she know it is really (their theirs)?

d. The stolen car is in (their theirs) garage. I think the car is (ours our).

e. That is (our ours) dog. Where is (yours your)?

3. Find the possessive pronouns in the grid. Write each in a sentence.

m	i	n	e	h
o	u	r	s	e
y	o	u	r	r
t	h	e	i	r

a. _____

b. _____

c. _____

d. _____

e. _____

Pronouns

Name _____   Grammar BLM **46**

Demonstrative pronouns take the place of and point out nouns. However, if the word is followed by a noun, it is not a demonstrative pronoun. It is a demonstrative adjective.

This is the train for Sydney.   demonstrative pronoun

This train is the train for Sydney.   demonstrative adjective

1. Circle the demonstrative pronouns. Underline the demonstrative adjectives.

   a. Those teachers are leaving.
   b. This is easy.
   c. These are very expensive.
   d. That is enough.
   e. These need to be cared for.
   f. That bus is going to Portland.
   g. These were given to me by Sam.
   h. That is an awful picture.

2. Write sentences of your own, using these words as demonstrative pronouns.

   | that | this | those | these |

   a. _____
   b. _____
   c. _____
   d. _____

3. Now write sentences using the same words as demonstrative adjectives.

   a. _____
   b. _____
   c. _____
   d. _____

Pronouns

Interrogative pronouns are used to ask questions. However, if the word is followed by a noun, it is not an interrogative pronoun. It is an interrogative adjective.

What is the time?   interrogative pronoun
What train is that?   interrogative adjective

1. Circle the interrogative pronouns. Underline the interrogative adjectives.

   a. What is going to happen next?

   b. Whose is it?

   c. What answer did you give?

   d. Which is the largest?

   e. Which bus will you catch?

   f. Who is that?

2. Write sentences of your own, using these words as interrogative pronouns.

   (who   whose   which   what)

   a. _____

   b. _____

   c. _____

   d. _____

3. Now write sentences using the same words as interrogative adjectives.

   a. _____

   b. _____

   c. _____

   d. _____

Conjunctions

Introduction

Conjunctions are words that are used to join words or groups of words.

> Examples: Peter *and* John rode their bikes.
> We did not go. We were ill. We did not go *because* we were ill.

There are different types of conjunctions. Fifth and sixth grade students should be able to recognize and use the following:

(a) **Coordinating conjunctions**—These join parts of a sentence that are of a similar type and of equal importance.

> Examples: I like fish *and* chips. (nouns linked)
> The dog ran across the yard *and* into its kennel. (two adverbial phrases linked)
> My team played well, *but* it was beaten. (two main clauses joined)

The most common coordinating conjunctions are the following:

> *and*   *but*   *for*   *nor*   *or*   *so*   *yet*

(b) **Subordinating conjunctions**—These are used to join a subordinate clause (adverb clause, adjective clause, noun clause) to the rest of the sentence.

> Example: We lost the match *because* we played badly.

Some common subordinating conjunctions follow:

after	*although*	*as*	*because*	*before*
once	*since*	*than*	*though*	*unless*
until	*when*	*whenever*	*where*	*wherever*

(c) **Correlative conjunctions**—These are conjunctions that are used in pairs.

> Examples: You can have *either* eggs *or* bacon for breakfast.
> She is *neither* tall *nor* short.
> Her brother is *both* handsome *and* intelligent.
> *Whether* it grows *or* not matters little.

Other correlative conjunctions follow:

> *as ... as*   *not only ... but also*   *not ... but*

Conjunctions usually occur between the things they are joining, but this is not always so. A sentence can begin with a conjunction:

> Example: *While in Sydney I visited the Opera House.*

In the past it was frowned upon to begin a sentence with *and* or *but*. Today it is acceptable to do so when you have good reason, such as for a particular effect.

> Example: *He found his keys. He found his car. He found his wallet. And he found happiness again.*

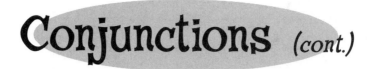
Conjunctions (cont.)

Teaching Strategies

What's your excuse?

Have children make up reasonable or crazy excuses for certain things.

I could not find my homework because Mom ate it.
I had to play football for the Oakland Raiders.
I went to the moon.

Edit and

To emphasize that some children overuse the conjunction *and*, write a passage on the chalkboard and have children suggest how it could be rewritten in a more interesting way.

I raced away quickly and out of the corner of my eye I saw a dog chasing me and it was barking loudly and I ran across the lawn and the dog followed after me and it was frothing at the mouth.

Brainstorm

Have children brainstorm pairs of phrases using *but* to join the two different ideas.
slow but steady   small but strong

They could also brainstorm pairs of words often associated with each other and joined with *and*.

Jack and Jill   bread and butter
steak and eggs   salt and pepper

Conjunctions

Name _____   Grammar BLM **48**

Conjunctions are joining words. They are used to join words and groups of words.

1. **Use the conjunctions in the box to complete the story.**

(yet   when   since   because   unless   and   although)

John thought about not going _____ it was so cold. He had not seen Bill _____ last December _____ they had met in the city one day. That day John _____ Bill had renewed their friendship. _____ John was older than Bill, the two boys still had a lot in common. John had been born two years before Bill, _____ they were both born on May 12. John decided he would go to see Bill _____ it started to snow.

2. **Use the conjunction *and* to pair each word in Box A with a word in Box B.**

Box A
(salt   knife   bread
up   round   thick
fish   oranges)

Box B
(pepper   chips   down
lemons   butter   thin
round   fork)

a. _____   e. _____
b. _____   f. _____
c. _____   g. _____
d. _____   h. _____

3. **Use a suitable conjunction to complete each sentence.**

a. I wanted to go to the movies, _____ I didn't have any money.

b. My parents were angry _____ I was two hours late.

c. He said I could have it _____ I gave him ten dollars.

d. Sally swept the floor, _____ I did the washing up.

e. You cannot leave _____ your room is tidy.

f. The match was still played _____ it was raining heavily.

Conjunctions

Conjunctions are joining words. They are used to join words and groups of words.

1. **Join the sentences by using the conjunction to begin the new sentence. Place a comma at the end of the introductory (first) clause.**

   a. We saw the bully coming. We began to run. (**when**)

   _____

   b. John did not try very hard. He did not pass the test. (**because**)

   _____

   c. You help me clean the room. I cannot come out to play. (**unless**)

   _____

   d. It was very hot. We still played soccer. (**although**)

   _____

   e. Tom boarded the school bus. He carried his skateboard. (**as**)

   _____

2. **Choose a word from the box to join the sentences. You might need to change the word order to make the new sentence. Place a comma at the end of an introductory clause.**

because	although	until

   a. The older boys arrive. We can do no more.

   _____

   b. The tree was not watered. It died last week.

   _____

   c. We still won the match. Our best player was missing.

   _____

   d. I will not give you any candy. You behave.

   _____

   e. The wheat crops were ruined. It hailed last week.

   _____

Conjunctions

Name _____ Grammar BLM **50**

Conjunctions are joining words. They are used to join words and groups of words.

1. Use a conjunction from the box to complete each sentence. Use each word once.

as	since	unless	but	because
if	although	and	until	when

a. I had not seen her _____ the middle of the year.

b. Sally could not come to the club _____ she was feeling ill.

c. The weather was cold _____ it was the middle of winter.

d. We left the classroom _____ the bell began to ring.

e. I swept the floor, _____ Tom set the table.

f. Our teacher will not help _____ you try hard.

g. Let's sit on the verandah _____ the sun sets.

h. We won the match _____ we were two players short.

i. Jon tried to kick a goal, _____ he missed.

j. We must go indoors _____ it begins to rain.

2. Choose your own conjunction to join the sentence in the box to each sentence below.

> Tommy stole the pie.

a. He was feeling hungry.

_____

b. He also stole a gold watch.

_____

c. He was left alone in the kitchen.

_____

d. He did not touch the cakes.

_____

e. He had never stolen anything before.

_____

Conjunctions

Conjunctions are joining words. They are used to join words and groups of words.

1. **Choose a pair of conjunctions from the box to complete each sentence.**

> both . . . and   as . . . as   either . . . or   whether . . . or
> not only . . . but also   neither . . . nor

a. You can have _____ eggs _____ bacon for breakfast.

b. She is _____ tall _____ short.

c. Her brother is _____ handsome _____ intelligent.

d. _____ it grows _____ not matters little.

e. Your homework is _____ late _____ messy!

f. I will leave _____ soon _____ Ben gets here.

2. **Write sentences of your own, using the following pairs of conjunctions.**

> both . . . and   not . . . but   whether . . . or   not only . . . but also

a. _____

b. _____

c. _____

d. _____

3. **Combine the sentences in three different ways, using three different conjunctions. Circle the conjunctions.**

a. The freeway was blocked by an accident. The traffic was held up.

_____

_____

_____

b. It was too cold to play outside. We looked over our sticker collections.

_____

_____

_____

Sentences

Introduction

A **sentence** is a group of words that makes sense and contains a subject and a verb. Take the example *into the box*. This is not a sentence as it does not have a subject and a verb and does not make sense by itself. A sentence begins with a capital letter and ends with a period, question mark, or exclamation mark.

There are four types of sentences.

(a) **Statements** simply state something or give information about something.
   Examples: *It is hot.*
   The time is eight o'clock.
   Koalas are marsupials.

(b) **Questions** ask something.
   Examples: *What is the weather like?*
   What time is it?
   What is a koala?

(c) **Commands** or **requests** direct someone to do something. They can also give advice or warnings.
   Examples: *Get out your books.*
   Sit up.
   Look out for sharp stones.

(d) **Exclamations** express the strong feeling of the speaker or writer about something.
   Examples: *Ouch!*
   I did it!
   What a full day!

Sentences can take several forms.

(a) **Simple sentences** consist of one clause. They can be divided into two parts: the **subject** tells who or what did something, and the **predicate** contains the verb and tells us what the subject did or is doing.
   Examples: *Horses (subject) run (predicate).*
   Billy (subject) climbed the tree (predicate).

• Sometimes a sentence does not seem to have a subject.
   Example: *Come here!*

In this case, even though the word is not actually said, the speaker is referring to *you* and really saying, *(You) come here!* The subject is understood.

(b) **Complex sentences** have more than one verb and thus have more than one clause. A complex sentence has at least one **main clause** (independent clause) and one or more **subordinate clauses** (dependent clauses).

Example: *When it was hot we went for a swim because we wanted to get cool.*

(c) **Compound sentences** consist of two or more main clauses (independent clauses) joined by a conjunction and, usually, a comma.

Example: *I washed the dishes, and Billy dried them.*

Speech can be reported directly or indirectly.

(a) **Direct speech** is the exact words spoken by a person. It is usually enclosed in quotation marks.

Example: *"I am writing a story," said Meg.*

Notice the quotation marks before the first word spoken and those after the last word spoken.

Now look at this sentence: *Mike said, "Look at this large dog."*

Here the unspoken words come first. Notice that the first word spoken begins with a capital letter.

The unspoken words can also come between the spoken words. This is sometimes called a broken quotation. For example, *"Come close to the fire," said Mike, "and warm your hands."*

Notice two pairs of quotation marks are used.

(b) **Indirect speech** reports a person's speech but does not necessarily quote the exact words used.

Examples: Direct speech: *"I am coming," said Paul.*

Indirect speech: *Paul said that he was coming.*

Teaching Strategies

Complete the sentence

Have children add words to complete a sentence. Informal exercises such as this demonstrate to children that a sentence must express a complete thought.

Bill has a new
I a rabbit

Jumbled sentences

Write a series of jumbled sentences on the chalkboard. Challenge children to orally unjumble them. As children become more confident, try giving longer sentences.

lives dog a kennel in a

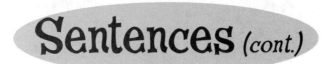

Sentences (cont.)

Complete the sentence

Have children complete sentences that you have begun or begin sentences that you have provided only the endings for. Activities such as this help children understand that sentences have a part that tells who or what did something and a part that tells what they did.

A spider . . .

A dog . . .

. . . swam across the creek.

. . . bit the boy on the leg.

Addo

Call out one word. Children must then add one word at a time to build a long, sensible sentence. This can be played as a circle game.

Bill

Bill ran

Bill ran across

Bill ran across the . . . and so on.

Subject/predicate match

On separate cards, write suitable subjects and predicates. Shuffle them and have children make sentences. Children can also make sets of cards for other groups to match.

The dog	*are in the garden.*
The girls	*is climbing the tree.*
The boy	*is chewing its bone.*

Make a sentence

Have children make up their own sentences from given words.

farmer	*sheep*	*meadow*

The farmer drove the sheep into the meadow.

Find the subject

Give children the opportunity to find the hidden subjects of given sentences. This will help them to realize that sentences can be written in different ways.

The girl raced across the lawn.

Across the lawn raced the girl.

Remind students that the easiest way to find the subject is to first locate the verb and then ask who or what is performing that action.

Sentences

A sentence is a group of words that expresses a complete thought. A sentence must make sense and must contain a subject and a verb.

1. After each of the following write *yes* if it expresses a complete thought. Write *no* if it does not express a complete thought.

   a. With both fists.   _____
   b. The boy chased the dog. _____
   c. In the middle of Australia._____
   d. Dogs bark loudly.   _____
   e. All her lunch.   _____

   f. The boys went home.   _____
   g. On top of the cupboard. _____
   h. If you drink that tea.   _____
   i. One day in July.   _____
   j. Mike caught three fish. _____

2. **Rearrange the words to make correct sentences.**

   a. bones to likes my dog chew

   _____

   b. a rose Ali picked the garden in

   _____

   c. a mammal whale is a

   _____

   d. weekend we camping are this going

   _____

3. **Add words of your own to make each of the following a complete sentence.**

   a. a koala can quickly

   _____

   b. the pilot the plane

   _____

   c. have a new

   _____

   d. the dog a bone

   _____

Sentences

A sentence has a part that tells who or what did something (subject) and a part that tells what the subject did (predicate).

1. **Add a subject to complete each sentence.**

   a. The _____ made its nest in the tall tree.

   b. A large _____ chased the rabbit into its burrow.

   c. Beside the house grew large _____.

   d. The little _____ ran happily across the playground.

   e. Along the valley stretched the large _____ .

   f. _____ inserted fifty cents into the machine.

2. **Add a predicate to complete each sentence.**

   a. The unhappy girl _____ .

   b. A large eagle _____ .

   c. The Murray River _____ .

   d. Cows _____ .

   e. My new shoes _____ .

   f. Many trees _____ .

3. **Draw a line to match each subject to its predicate.**

   a. The brave fireman   was a famous dancer and actor.

   b. All of the water   were herded into the yards.

   c. Gold   rescued the children.

   d. Gene Kelly   has evaporated.

   e. The buffaloes   was discovered in Alaska.

   f. The beautiful necklace   are found in Egypt.

   g. The pyramids   are native to Australia.

   h. Kangaroos and wallabies   was made of silver.

Sentences

There are four types of sentences: statements, questions, commands or requests, and exclamations.

1. **After each sentence, write** *statement, question, command,* **or** *exclamation.*

   a. Where did John go? _____

   b. What a lovely day! _____

   c. Sit up! _____

   d. A magpie is black and white. _____

   e. I lost my wallet yesterday. _____

   f. Move that chair, please. _____

   g. Why did the bell ring early? _____

   h. It's hot! _____

2. **Write different types of sentences.**

   a. Write 2 statements about school.

   _____

   _____

   b. Write 2 questions you would like to ask an alien.

   _____

   _____

   c. Write 2 commands you might give a pet.

   _____

   _____

   d. Write 2 exclamations you might make at a football game.

   _____

   _____

Sentences

There are four types of sentences: statements, questions, commands or requests, and exclamations.

1. **Write a possible question to match each answer statement.**

    a. _____

    It is black and white.

    b. _____

    It is nearly seven o'clock.

    c. _____

    A beetle has six legs.

    d. _____

    The smallest bird is the hummingbird.

    e. _____

    His name is Rover.

    f. _____

    There are 22 children.

2. **Write a statement to answer each question.**

    a. What color is a penguin?

    _____

    b. Where do you live?

    _____

    c. When do the next holidays begin?

    _____

    d. What is a seagull?

    _____

    e. What is your favorite animal?

    _____

    f. Where is the city of Seoul?

    _____

Sentences

Name _____ Grammar BLM 56

A simple sentence is made up of one clause. It contains a subject and a verb and makes sense on its own. A compound sentence is made up of two or more main clauses joined by a conjunction and, usually, a comma.

Simple sentences: *I washed the dishes.*

Compound sentence: *I washed the dishes, and Bill dried them.*

1. Rewrite each pair of simple sentences as a compound sentence.

   a. Mike tried to rescue his dog from the pool. Mike fell in.

   _____

   b. John switched on the oven. He made a cake.

   _____

   c. Pam went to the beach. She did not go for a swim.

   _____

   d. Mom cut the lawn. I raked up the clippings.

   _____

2. Add another main clause to make a compound sentence.

   a. Sally went to the beach, but _____ .

   b. A terrier won first prize, and _____ .

   c. You can go to the movies, or _____ .

   d. The pies are popular, and _____ .

3. Circle the two main clauses in each of these compound sentences.

   a. Mike tried to jump the fence, but he slipped and fell.

   b. Mr. Smith lives in Dallas, and he also has a house in Aspen.

   c. Mike and Terry went into the garden, and they picked some flowers.

   d. You can have a pie, or you can have a pizza.

Sentences

A **simple** sentence is made up of one clause. It contains a subject and a verb and makes sense on its own. *I washed the dishes.*

A **compound** sentence is made up of two or more main clauses joined by a conjunction and, usually, a comma. *I washed the dishes, and Bill dried them.*

A **complex** sentence is made up of a main clause and a subordinate or dependent clause. *I saw the lady who broke the eggs.*

1. Write *simple*, *compound*, or *complex* after each sentence.

   a. I found my trunks, and I went to the pool. _____

   b. We must wait here until the rain stops. _____

   c. The winning girl accepted the prize. _____

   d. Mike found silver, but he did not find gold. _____

   e. The concert was held in the old hall. _____

   f. Sam did not come because he was ill. _____

2. **Complete these to make complex sentences.**

   a. The farmer did not harvest the crop _____ .

   b. We stayed with John _____ .

   c. The girl _____ is my best friend.

   d. Peter visited the farm _____ .

   e. I saw the man _____ .

   f. We did not go swimming _____ .

   g. There is the dog _____ .

   h. The boy _____ catches my bus.

Sentences

Direct speech is the exact words spoken by a person. The words are usually enclosed in quotation marks.
"I am writing a story," said Meg.
Indirect speech reports a person's speech but does not necessarily quote the exact words used. The words are not enclosed in quotation marks.
Paul said that he was coming.

1. **Add the correct punctuation to show direct speech.**

   a. Have you been to New Orleans asked Bill.

   b. Come and help me shouted Sam.

   c. The trip was tiring he said I was glad when I arrived.

   d. It's nearly lunchtime shouted Mom. We'll have some fish and chips.

   e. You can travel all the way by bus the teacher told us and the scenery is beautiful.

   f. Tom said We should leave before six o'clock.

2. **Rewrite each sentence as indirect speech.**

   a. "I would like to go on a picnic," said Tom.

   _____

   b. "Where are we going?" asked Kate.

   _____

   c. "What time is it?" inquired Fred.

   _____

   d. "I can't wait for Christmas," she said.

   _____

   e. I asked, "How far is the river from here?"

   _____

   f. "Are they going with us?" she asked.

   _____

Prepositional Phrases

Introduction

A **phrase** is a group of words without a subject and predicate. It functions as a single part of speech. A **prepositional phrase** consists of a preposition, a noun or pronoun that is its object, and any modifiers of the noun or pronoun.

    Examples: Jon ate *at home.*   Jon ate *at the luxurious convalescent home.*

Prepositional phrases function as adjectives (to modify nouns and pronouns) and as adverbs (to modify verbs, adjectives, and adverbs).

(a) **Adjectival prepositional phrases** tell us more about or describe a noun or pronoun. They should be placed close to the noun or pronoun they modify. Example: The girl *with long hair* is coming to the party.

(b) **Adverbial prepositional phrases** do the work of adverbs. They tell us more about verbs, adjectives, or adverbs. They tell us how, when, or where an action occurs.

    Examples: The boy kicked the ball *with a lot of skill.* (modifies verb "kicked")
               Sally was rich *as a queen.* (modifies adjective "rich")
               I run early *in the morning.* (modifies adverb "early")

Teaching Strategies

Circle the phrases

Have children search through a photocopy of a familiar story to find and circle the prepositional phrases. They could color-code the circles to identify the phrases as adjectival or adverbial.

Suggest a phrase

Have children suggest adverbial or adjectical prepositional phrases to complete sentences.

The school bell rings at nine o'clock.
I saw the girl with red hair.

Add a phrase

Have children add prepositional phrases of their own to make sentences more interesting.

We left the house.   *We left the house before noon.*
The girl fed the puppy.   *The girl with red hair fed the puppy.*

Where should the phrase go?

Make up a number of sentences in which the phrase has been incorrectly placed. Have children rewrite the sentences correctly.

Prepositional Phrases

Name _____   Grammar BLM **59**

A phrase is a group of words that has no subject and verb.

1. Write sentences of your own that begin or end with these prepositional phrases.

   a. On a hot day _____ .

   b. After the grape harvest _____ .

   c. Near the deserted town _____ .

   d. _____ until the bell rings.

   e. _____ with lots of courage.

   f. _____ before daylight.

2. Draw a line to match the prepositional phrases that have similar meanings.

   a. after twelve o'clock   in the rear

   b. with fear and trembling   in a frightened manner

   c. at the back   before noon

   d. during the morning   in the afternoon

3. Draw a line to match the prepositional phrases that have opposite meanings.

   a. after twelve o'clock   in the backyard

   b. in the classroom   in a cowardly way

   c. with great courage   before the sowing

   d. after the harvest   with slow carefulness

   e. at great speed   on the playground

   f. on the front lawn   in the morning

   g. for several hours   only a split second

Prepositional Phrases

A phrase is a group of words that has no subject and verb. Some prepositional phrases do the work of an adjective. They describe or add meaning to a noun or pronoun.

The girl <u>with red hair</u> is my sister.

1. **Circle the adjectival prepositional phrase in each sentence.**

   a. The dog with long ears is mine.

   b. The man with a guilty conscience is unhappy.

   c. The spire on the old church was damaged by the wind.

   d. The house on the hill belongs to us.

   e. The girl in the green dress is my sister.

   f. That table in the kitchen is old.

2. **Circle the noun each underlined prepositional phrase describes.**

   a. The aircraft <u>with black wings</u> is above us.

   b. The child <u>across the yard</u> is my nephew.

   c. That building <u>near the cliff</u> is falling down.

   d. The house <u>in the valley</u> is made of pine logs.

   e. The skyscraper <u>in this street</u> was built by my uncle.

   f. The church <u>with the cross</u> was built last year.

3. **Write an adjectival prepositional phrase to describe each noun.**

   a. the cat _____

   b. the whale _____

   c. the classroom _____

   d. the teacher _____

   e. the sandwich _____

   f. the backpack _____

Prepositional Phrases

A phrase is a group of words that has no subject and verb. Some prepositional phrases do the work of an adverb. They tell how, when, or where an action happens.
We walked <u>into the classroom</u>.

1. **Circle the adverbial prepositional phrase in each sentence.**

   a. We are going to England.

   b. The watchmaker worked with great care.

   c. I put the toys in the box.

   d. She spoke in an angry way.

   e. I held the injured bird in my hand.

   f. After a short pause we continued the search.

2. **Circle the verb each underlined prepositional phrase tells more about.**

   a. Dad walked <u>through the house</u>.

   b. The boy ran <u>in the marathon</u>.

   c. I jumped <u>into my costume</u>.

   d. I was working <u>on the boat</u>.

   e. I listened <u>to the radio</u>.

   f. We pushed <u>on the button</u>.

3. **Write an adverbial prepositional phrase to complete each sentence. Each phrase should begin with a preposition and answer the question in parentheses.**

   a. We saw the birds _____ . (where?)

   b. I threw the stone _____ . (why?)

   c. Last Saturday we walked _____ . (where?)

   d. We left the movies _____ . (when?)

   e. The motorist drove _____ . (how?)

   f. The teacher spoke to me _____ . (how?)

Clauses

Introduction

A **clause** is a group of words that contains a subject and a predicate. The subject of a clause may be expressed or understood.

There are two types of clauses.
(a) A **main clause** (independent clause) contains the main thought of the sentence and makes sense standing alone.
  Examples: *I spoke to the teacher* who is our football coach.
  The dog that was barking *chased me across the lawn.*

(b) A **subordinate clause** (dependent clause) cannot make sense standing on its own. To make a sentence, a subordinate clause must be added to a main clause.
  Examples: I saw the dog *when I came home.*
  They went to the store *so they could buy ice cream.*

Subordinate clauses add information to a sentence and function in the same way as *adjectives*, *adverbs*, or *nouns*.
  Examples: The woman *who received the prize* is my mother. (adjective)
  Our class stops working *when the bell rings.* (adverb)
  I think *that we should always do the right thing.* (noun)

Sentences are analyzed by finding and naming the clauses.
(a) **Simple sentences** consist of one clause.
  Example: *Horses run.*

(b) **Complex sentences** have more than one subject-verb combination and thus have more than one clause. A complex sentence has at least one main clause and one or more subordinate clauses. A subordinate clause is introduced by a subordinating conjunction or a relative pronoun.
  Example: I was resting *while he was swimming laps.*

(c) **Compound sentences** consist of two or more main clauses (independent clauses) joined by a conjunction.
  Example: *I washed the dishes, and Billy dried them.*

Teaching Strategies
The main thing
Provide students with practice in finding the main clause in a sentence by having them search through a photocopy of a familiar story, circling the main clauses. Remind them that a main clause can stand alone and contains the main thought of the sentence. Point out that a simple sentence is, in fact, one main clause.

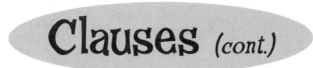

Clauses (cont.)

Main clause beep

Have children sit in a circle. Choose a child to say a word to start a clause. Each child in turn then adds a word to build a main clause. When the clause is complete, the next child says "Beep." The game can be extended to add a subordinate clause to the main clause.

Act the clause

Organize children in groups of four. Tell groups that the first child is to provide a verb, the second child is to provide a subject, the third child is to arrange the verb and subject to make a clause, and the fourth child is to act out the clause. Ensure that all children get a turn in each role.

Clause match-up

Have children match main clauses to subordinate clauses. This is also an excellent reading activity.

These are the brave boys   *because he was feeling ill.*
Bill did not come   *where the bus stop was.*
The bus driver didn't know   *who rescued the drowning child.*

Clause call-out

Write a main clause on the chalkboard and challenge children to call out appropriate subordinate clauses.

We went to the park   *when we had eaten lunch.*
                               where the banana tree grows.
                               because we wanted to play.

Verb search

Write some clauses on the chalkboard. Have children search for and identify the verb in each clause.

I saw the boy who broke the glass.

Add the verb

Have children orally add missing verbs to clauses.

I saw the boy who ten goals.
I saw the boy who kicked ten goals.
The police arrested the thief who the jewels.
The police arrested the thief who stole the jewels.

Clauses

A clause is a group of words that contains a verb and its subject. A main clause contains the main thought of the sentence and makes sense standing alone. A subordinate clause (dependent clause) does not make sense standing on its own. It adds information to the main clause.

1. Draw a line to match each main clause to its subordinate clause.

Main clause	Subordinate clause
a. Where is the book	where the railroad station was.
b. Here is the burglar	if we get any hail.
c. I asked the stranger	because her uncle has arrived.
d. The grape crop will be damaged	which has yellow blossoms on it.
e. Winter is the season	that I read yesterday?
f. Sally would not come with us	whose dog bit the policeman.
g. I know the man	who was arrested by the police.
h. This is the tree	when the snow begins to fall.

2. Underline the main clause and circle the subordinate clause in each sentence. Hint: The main clause might be in two parts with the subordinate clause between them.

   a. The student who stayed away from school was punished.

   b. The lady who is in charge of the school spoke to the teachers.

   c. I broke the bottle that had juice in it.

   d. The farm where the grapes are grown belongs to my uncle.

   e. The shed that houses the equipment was burned to the ground.

   f. The cupboard that is used to store glasses is made of mahogany.

   g. The food that is fit to be eaten is in the refrigerator.

   h. We visited the place where stone is mined.

Clauses

A clause is a group of words that contains a verb and its subject. Subordinate clauses add information to a sentence and function in the same way as adjectives, adverbs, or nouns.

The woman *who received the prize* is my mother. (adjective)
Our class stops working *when the bell rings*. (adverb)
I think *that we should always do the right thing*. (noun)

1. **Draw lines to match each main clause with an adjectival subordinate clause.**

   a. The farmer found the dogs   which began Easter Day

   b. Our holiday . . . was very restful.   that likes to chase its tail.

   c. We admired the garden   whose father is from Paris.

   d. I spoke to the boy   that killed the sheep.

   e. I have a new puppy   which is in the museum

   f. The dinosaur . . . was found by Sam.   which was planted in spring.

2. **Complete each sentence by completing each adjectival subordinate clause.**

   a. This is the girl <u>who</u> _____ .

   b. The old cow <u>which</u> _____ looked sick.

   c. The picture <u>which</u> _____ was painted by my friend.

   d. The old lady <u>who</u> _____ makes great pizzas.

   e. The brave girl <u>who</u> _____ was awarded a medal.

   f. I caught the pigeon <u>that</u> _____ .

3. **Complete each sentence by adding an adjectival subordinate clause.**

   a. Sally found a wallet _____ .

   b. We switched off the music _____ .

   c. I showed John the knife _____ .

   d. I told her to throw away the shirt _____ .

Clauses

A clause is a group of words that contains a verb and its subject. Subordinate clauses add information to a sentence and function in the same way as adjectives, adverbs, or nouns.

The woman *who received the prize* is my mother. (adjective)
Our class stops working *when the bell rings.* (adverb)
I think *that we should always do the right thing.* (noun)

1. Circle the verb that each underlined subordinate clause tells us more about.

   a. She can climb a tree <u>as a monkey does</u>.

   b. I punished Spot <u>because he chewed my new shoe</u>.

   c. Meet me <u>where the water pipe burst</u>.

   d. <u>After we have had lunch</u>, we are going to the movies.

   e. No spectators are allowed <u>while a rehearsal is in progress</u>.

   f. They were asleep <u>before the sun had set</u>.

2. Underline the adverbial subordinate clause in each sentence. On the line, write whether it tells us *how, when, where,* or *why* the action of the verb took place.

   a. I went swimming because it was hot. _____

   b. The girls played where there were trees. _____

   c. You may dress as you wish. _____

   d. We left the classroom when the bell rang. _____

   e. As our captain is sick, we must choose another player. _____

   f. Accidents often happen where two roads cross. _____

3. Draw a line to match each main clause with an adverbial subordinate clause.

   a. We must play inside   because he could not find his uniform.

   b. John spoke   where the roads meet.

   c. Mike did not come   since she left to live in the city.

   d. I haven't seen Janet   even though we will be late.

   e. We must wash the dishes   until the rain stops.

   f. The accident happened   as if he were very nervous.

Clauses

A clause is a group of words that contains a verb and its subject. Subordinate clauses add information to a sentence and function in the same way as adjectives, adverbs, or nouns.

The woman *who received the prize* is my mother. (adjective)

Our class stops working *when the bell rings*. (adverb)

I think *that we should always do the right thing*. (noun)

1. **Look at each underlined subordinate clause. Write whether it is an adjective clause, an adverb clause, or a noun clause.**

    a. The cup <u>that is on the shelf</u> belongs to Tom.   _____

    b. <u>What he said</u> is truly a lie.   _____

    c. Egypt is a land <u>that has lots of pyramids</u>.   _____

    d. Tom did not ride his bike <u>because it had a flat tire</u>.   _____

    e. Ned cleaned his teeth <u>after he had eaten</u>.   _____

    f. The witness stated <u>that she recognized the man</u>.   _____

    g. We left the party <u>when the music began</u>.   _____

    h. <u>After they had eaten their lunch</u>, they played games.   _____

2. **Add the type of subordinate clause asked for in parentheses.**

    a. The scouts camped _____ . (adverb)

    b. Australia is a land _____ . (adjective)

    c. Mike washed his hands_____ . (adverb)

    d. Sally did not come _____ . (adverb)

    e. _____ they played games. (adverb)

    f. The truth is _____ . (noun)

    g. _____ is not true. (noun)

    h. The police are searching for a man _____ . (adjective)

Clauses

An adjectival clause should be placed next to, or as close as possible to, the noun or pronoun it is describing.

1. **Rewrite each of these sentences so they make more sense.**

   a. I bought the tiger from the lady <u>that had black and gold stripes</u>.

   _____

   b. The baby was picked up by the old man <u>who had a pacifier in his mouth</u>.

   _____

   c. The teacher spoke to the little boy <u>who is married with two children</u>.

   _____

   d. The train is in the station <u>that arrived late</u>.

   _____

   e. The bull gored the man <u>that has two large horns</u>.

   _____

   f. In front of the house is an oak tree <u>which has a red roof</u>.

   _____

2. **Join the two sentences so that the new sentence contains an adjective clause.**

   a. This is the dog. The dog attacked the stranger.

   _____

   b. This is the girl. The girl lives next door to me.

   _____

   c. The children hurried past the old house. The house was said to be haunted.

   _____

   d. The big gum tree has been cut down. It stood in our backyard.

   _____

   e. The boy won a silver medal. I knew the boy well.

   _____

   f. The family was cared for by friends. Their home was destroyed by fire.

   _____

Clauses

Sentences can have more than one subordinate clause.

1. **Use the following clauses to complete the sentences below. Write the numbers in the spaces.**

1	who caught the thief	7	who were unarmed
2	where the thief had hidden them	8	that were very hungry
3	that had broken a wing	9	who live in our street
4	that was growing in our backyard	10	that my father drives
5	who was playing soccer	11	who was sitting in the front seat
6	when the ball hit him	12	where he could leave his bag

a. I found the bird _____ in a tall tree _____ .

b. The hunters _____ were attacked by wolves _____ .

c. The policeman _____ found the jewels _____ .

d. Tom _____ asked the teacher _____ .

e. The boy _____ hurt his head _____ .

f. Many people _____ like the car _____ .

2. **Complete each sentence by adding subordinate clauses of your own. The words to begin each clause are given.**

a. The man <u>who</u> _____ fell <u>when</u> _____ .

b. The river <u>that</u> _____ was swum by the girl <u>who</u> _____ .

c. The birds <u>that</u> _____ were shot by the hunter <u>who</u> _____ .

d. The boy <u>who</u> _____ did not play <u>because</u> _____ .

e. The girls <u>who</u> _____ waited <u>until</u> _____ .

f. The player <u>whose</u> _____ kicked the goal <u>that</u> _____ .

g. The teacher <u>who</u> _____ laughed <u>when</u> _____ .

Punctuation

Introduction

An easy way to draw children's attention to the importance of punctuation is to make an analogy to the road signs we must obey.

A stop sign signals to a motorist that she must stop and not proceed until everything is clear. A period tells us we must stop a moment so that sentences do not run into each other and become difficult to understand. A yield sign tells a motorist to pause to ensure the traffic has passed. A comma tells us to pause to ensure the sentence makes sense. If all motorists obey the traffic signs, then cars, trucks, and bikes will travel along streets safely. If we all obey the punctuation signals, then we will be able to convey our thoughts and ideas clearly.

The main elements of punctuation that fifth and sixth grade students should develop a working knowledge of are as follows.

A **capital letter** is used

(a) for the first letter of a sentence.

(b) for the first letter of a person's given name and family name.

(c) for the pronoun *I*.

(d) for the first letter of names of the days of the week, months of the year, and special times such as *Easter*, *Christmas*.

(e) for the first letter of names of towns, cities, countries, streets, schools, etc.

(f) sometimes to begin each line in poetry.

(g) for the first letter of the main words in the titles of books, poems, songs, and television programs.

A **period** is used

(a) at the end of a statement or command sentence.
   Examples: *That dog is brown.* (statement)
   Sit down. (command)

(b) in abbreviations.
   Examples:

etc.	*Maj.*	*St.*	*Calif.*
Capt.	*Col.*	*Lt. Gov.*	*Tex.*
abbr.	*Dr.*	*Sen.*	
Mr.	*Pres.*	*Eng.*	
Ave.	*Ms.*	*Sp.*	
Mrs.	*Rd.*	*Ger.*	
Prof.	*Supt.*	*Fla.*	

Punctuation (cont.)

A **question mark** is used at the end of a sentence that is a direct question. It might be helpful to point out the question indicators *who, when, where, why, what,* and *how.*

> *What is the time?* (direct question)
> *I asked her what time it was.* (indirect question)

An **exclamation point** is used at the end of a sentence that expresses a strong emotion. Point out to children that exclamation sentences are often short.

> Examples: *Wow!   Ouch!   Well done!*

Remind children to use only one exclamation point. Using more than one does not create greater emphasis.

A **comma** is used

(a) to separate words in a list.

> Examples: *Please go to the store and buy oranges, bread, milk, and butter.*
> (separate nouns)
> *It was a big, black, hairy spider.* (separate adjectives)
> *Please work quickly, neatly, and quietly.* (separate adverbs)

(b) after the salutation in a friendly letter.

> Example: *Dear Katy,*

(c) at the close of a letter, before signing your name.

> Example: *Yours faithfully,*

(d) to separate direct speech from the rest of the sentence.

> Example: *"I hope he will be here soon," said Mike.*

(e) to separate two or more adjectives or adverbs.

> Examples: *Susan is a fast, accurate, cheerful worker.*
> *The cat slowly, silently, skillfully moved in on the mouse.*

(f) sometimes to separate a connective from the rest of the sentence if the connective is used to begin the sentence.

> Example: *So, they went to the movies in the afternoon.*

(g) sometimes to separate a beginning phrase or clause from the rest of the sentence.

> Example: *In the cool of the evening, we will have a picnic.*

(h) to separate embedded phrases and clauses from the rest of the sentence.

> Example: *Ms. Jackson, our new music teacher, used to play in a band.*

Punctuation (cont.)

Quotation marks are used to enclose direct speech (the words actually spoken by someone).

  Examples: *Ali asked, "When are we going?"* *"Let's go now," said Ben.*

A **hyphen** is used

(a) to form compound adjectives, adverbs, and nouns.

  Examples: the *blackish-blue* fish (adj.) *one-half* empty (adv.)
      half-moon (n.)

(b) when the main word of a compound starts with a capital letter.

  Example: *un-American*

(c) to avoid confusion with another word.

  Examples: *re-cover (fit with a new cover)*
      recover (return to normal)

A **dash** is used

(a) to mark a change of thought or an abrupt turn in the sentence or to indicate faltering speech.

  Example: *You can't do that—oh, you can.*

(b) to indicate an unfinished or interrupted sentence.

  Example: *But, Sir, I thought—*

(c) to enclose extra information. (Parentheses can also be used for this.)

  Example: *Somewhere in Australia—I'm not sure of the exact spot—is a large deposit of gold.*

A **colon** is used to introduce more information. The information may be a list, words, phrases, clauses, or a quotation.

  Example: *He bought lots of fruit: apples, pineapple, and watermelon.*

A **semicolon** is used

(a) to join two short, linked sentences.

  Example: *I like jelly; my sister prefers ice cream.*

(b) to separate complex lists.

  Example: *She brought with her a jacket with a hood; a coat with big pockets, a fur collar, and a matching scarf; and a large umbrella.*

An **apostrophe** is used

(a) in contractions to indicate where letters have been omitted.

  Example: *I will*   *I'll*

(b) to indicate possession in nouns.

  Examples: *a dog's kennel* *the three dogs' kennels*

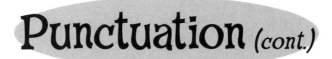

Punctuation *(cont.)*

Teaching Strategies

Beep marks
Make cards that have large punctuation marks written on them. Read a simple story aloud to the children. Whenever you reach a punctuation mark, say "Beep!" The children must then hold up the missing mark.

What's the meaning?
From time to time challenge children by writing a piece on the chalkboard in which the meaning may be altered by different or no punctuation.

Have you eaten Bill?   *Have you eaten, Bill?*
I have forty-two dollar coins.   *I have forty two-dollar coins.*
Sally is a pretty, kind person.   *Sally is a pretty kind person.*
He ate a half-fried chicken.   *He ate a half fried chicken.*
I left him convinced he was a fool. *I left him, convinced he was a fool.*

What a joke
Give children plenty of practice punctuating by writing unpunctuated jokes or riddles on the chalkboard. Have individual children add the punctuation in color.
what cat lives in the sea
an octopus

Read aloud
Have individual children read aloud their own writing efforts while other children suggest necessary punctuation.

Punctuation

Name _____

A capital letter is used for
- **the first letter of a sentence.**
- **the first letter in names—people, places, pets, days, months, countries, states, towns, mountains, rivers.**
- **the pronoun I.**

1. Color the boxes that contain words that should begin with a capital letter.

michelle	swan lake	plate	christmas	beetles
south	uranus	october	canada	mount everest
england	asia	pacific ocean	tables	london
wednesday	summer	easter	kansas city	rialto house
stranger	shamrock hotel	vietnam	murray river	wattle street

2. Complete the sentences.

a. My given name is _____ .

b. My birthday is in the month of _____ .

c. The street I live on is _____ .

d. The school I attend is _____ .

e. My teacher's name is _____ .

f. I live in the town or city of _____ .

g. The country I would most like to visit is _____ .

3. Rewrite the following sentences correctly.

a. last saturday julie went to chicago

_____

b. at christmas we are going to italy which is a country in europe

_____

c. the wedding will take place at st patrick's church in greensboro

_____

Punctuation

Commas are used to show short pauses in writing. They are used in various ways, including separating nouns, separating adjectives, and after introductory clauses and phrases.

1. **Complete each sentence by using words from the box. Don't forget to use commas.**

scissors	roses	ash	daffodils	eucalyptus
wheat	skunks	pliers	hammers	penguins
rice	zebras	sycamore	corn	hyacinths

a. _____ are cereals.

b. _____ are flowers.

c. _____ are black and white.

d. _____ are tools.

e. _____ are trees.

2. **Each sentence contains a phrase that needs to be set off with commas. The first one has been done for you.**

a. Adelaide, the capital of South Australia, is a beautiful city.

b. Anders Celsius a Swedish astronomer introduced the Celsius scale in 1742.

c. The South Pole a featureless spot in a freezing wilderness was first reached by Amundsen.

d. The toothbrush according to a 17th century encyclopedia was first invented in China in 1498.

e. Ian one of this class's finest writers has won first prize in the poetry contest.

f. Interpol the first international crime fighting organization was formed in 1923 in Paris.

Punctuation

An apostrophe is used
- **in contractions to indicate where letters have been omitted.**
  I'll (I will)
- **to indicate possession in nouns.**
  a dog's kennel
  the three dogs' kennels

1. **Write in full what the following contractions mean.**

   a. hasn't _____   e. we'll _____

   b. we've _____   f. can't _____

   c. o'clock _____   g. 'tis _____

   d. didn't _____   h. 'twas _____

2. **Write the following as contractions.**

   a. I am _____   f. you have _____

   b. I have _____   g. who is _____

   c. I would _____   h. it is _____

   d. I shall _____   i. he is _____

   e. could not _____   j. were not _____

3. **Add apostrophes where they are needed.**

Thats the place well go. Theres bound to be lots of fish. Its a really

good spot. Were lucky youd seen it before. Theyre going to be

jealous when they know weve got it. Theyll probably say theyre not

coming now.

Punctuation

An apostrophe is used
- **in contractions to indicate where letters have been omitted.**
  I'll (I will)
- **to indicate possession in nouns.**
  a dog's kennel
  the three dogs' kennels

1. **Add apostrophes where they are needed.**

   a. The policemans helmet fell on the ground.

   b. I fastened the dogs collar around its neck.

   c. My mothers car is in the garage.

   d. The clocks hands pointed to midday.

   e. The elephants tusk was taken by the hunter.

   f. The childs foot slipped on the step.

2. **Add apostrophes where they are needed.**

   a. The ladies hats are on the bed.

   b. The childrens toys are in the box.

   c. The cows tails swished about like fly swatters.

   d. My sisters bedrooms are next to each other.

   e. The cities skyscrapers are always a beautiful sight.

   f. The eagles beaks were sharp and curved.

3. **Rewrite these phrases, making use of apostrophes. The first one has been done for you.**

   a. the ears of the horse   the horse's ears

   b. the boots of the soldier   _____

   c. the hats of the men   _____

   d. the tail of the tiger   _____

   e. the books of the teacher   _____

   f. the red noses of the clowns   _____

Punctuation

Name _____   Grammar BLM **72**

An exclamation point is used at the end of a sentence that expresses a strong emotion. Exclamatory sentences are nearly always short.

1. **Rewrite the following sentences as exclamations. Use only one, two, or three words.**

    a. The stove is on fire, and I am afraid the house might burn down.

    _____

    b. I want you to be fast.

    _____

    c. I need your help urgently and straight away.

    _____

    d. You must hold on tightly, or you will be thrown off.

    _____

    e. Watch where you are going because a large truck is about to hit you.

    _____

    f. Our team has just scored a goal.

    _____

2. **Write exclamation points, question marks, or periods where they are needed.**

    a. What a great movie I really like the end What big sharks
    b. Did you see the spider Look out There could be one on your hat
    c. What a lovely day Look at those waves Wow
    d. Yuk How horrible Would you believe it

3. **Write exclamations beginning with the following words.**

    a. How   _____
    b. What   _____
    c. If only _____
    d. How   _____
    e. What   _____
    f. If only _____

Punctuation

A semicolon is used to join two short, linked sentences or to separate complex lists.

1. **Add commas or semicolons in the correct places.**

   a. It was nearly Christmas so we looked for presents.

   b. I was really exhausted I had never run so far.

   c. Mr. Smith is a good teacher but you need to listen to him carefully.

   d. Football is a winter sport baseball is a summer sport.

   e. Lisa was the teacher's first choice she was quiet intelligent and a hard worker.

   f. On our visit to the zoo we saw zebras grazing in a pen lots of snakes in the snakepit seals their babies and a diver in the pool and an elephant in its enclosure.

A colon is used to introduce more information. The information may be a list, words, phrases, clauses, or a quotation.

2. **Add commas or colons in the correct places.**

   a. These are my favorite foods hamburgers pies candy and apples.

   b. This is what he said "The United States flag is red white and blue."

   c. Get these things books pens papers pencils and crayons.

   d. The instructions read as follows "Wash lightly in cold water."

A dash is used to mark a change of thought or an abrupt turn in the sentence, to indicate an unfinished or interrupted sentence, or to enclose extra information.

3. Write three sentences of your own in which dashes are used.

   a. _____

   b. _____

   c. _____

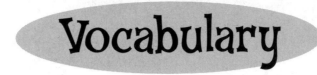
Vocabulary

Introduction

Grammar is also concerned with the way an overall text is structured to engage an audience and to deliver its message and with the way we choose particular words appropriate to that audience and message. It is important to generate an interest in words and to encourage children to be thoughtful about the words they use. If students develop an interest in language at an early age, they should continue to appreciate throughout their school life and into adulthood the richness and diversity of our ever-growing language.

Concepts students should become familiar with are as follows:

Antonyms

An antonym is a word that has the opposite meaning to another word.
Example: *absent/present*

Synonyms

A synonym is a word that has the same or a similar meaning to another word. Help children to understand that writers choose their words carefully and that one word may be more appropriate than another in a given situation.
Example: *wed/marry*

Homonyms

There are two types.

(a) A **homophone** is a word that sounds the same as another word but has a different meaning and different spelling.
   Examples: *bear/bare*   *sun/son*

(b) A **homograph** is a word that is spelled the same as another word but has a different meaning.
   Examples: *I fished from the <u>bank</u> of the river.*
   I cashed the check at the <u>bank</u>.
   I don't think you should <u>bank</u> on it too much.

Anagrams

An anagram is a word that contains exactly the same letters as another word—but in a different arrangement.
Examples: *palm/lamp*   *flow/wolf*

Compound words

These are sometimes called joined words. They are simply a large word made up of two or more smaller words. The combinations can be a noun and noun (shell + fish = shellfish) or an adjective and a noun (black + bird = blackbird).

Twin words

These are words that are often paired together, especially in speech.
Example: *salt and pepper*

Vocabulary *(cont.)*

Similes
A simile is a figure of speech that compares one thing with another. It is a direct comparison introduced by the words *like* or *as*.
Examples: *Her hair was like spun gold.*
The pavement was as hot as fire.

Metaphors
A metaphor is an implied comparison. Rather than saying one thing is *like* another, a metaphor says that one thing is another.
Example: *The clouds were full sacks ready to burst.*

Root words, prefixes, and suffixes
It is often helpful to see a word in terms of its various parts. These parts are called the root, the prefix, and the suffix.

The **root word** is the word from which other words are built.
Example: *kind*

A **prefix** is a group of letters placed at the beginning of a word. It often makes the word mean its opposite.
Example: *un + kind = unkind*

A **suffix** is a group of letters added to the end of a word. (Sometimes spelling changes have to be made.)

Example: *unkindly:*   *un*   *kind*   *ly*
                     prefix   root   suffix

Teaching Strategies

Homophone hunt
Write a list of words on the chalkboard. Challenge students to think of the corresponding homophones. They can also create cartoons to illustrate the homophones.

allowed/aloud	*ate/eight*	*eye/I*	*bare/bear*
bean/been	*blew/blue*	*board/bored*	*brake/break*
flea/flee	*hear/here*	*knit/nit*	*one/won*
pair/pear	*sun/son*		

Fish
On blank playing cards write pairs of synonyms, antonyms, or homophones. Encourage children to play "Go Fish" with them.

Scattered letters
Write a selection of letters scattered on the chalkboard. Have children think of as many words as they can using the letters. Make the game more challenging by introducing a timer.

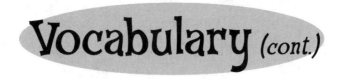
Vocabulary (cont.)

Word collection

Organize a word collection bulletin board in the classroom. Encourage children to find, collect, and then display words on the board. The board could have a number of different headings, such as Interesting Words, Words That Sound Funny, Words That Sound Like Noises, Words That Sound Important. Ask children to think of other headings they would like to use.

Tongue twisters

Challenge children to say a tongue twister quickly. Then have them make up their own tongue twisters for their friends to try.
She sells seashells by the seashore.

Odd words

Have children search for words with interesting or unusual features. Here are some to start them off.

hijinks:	*three dotted letters in a row*
strength:	*eight letters but only one vowel*
subbookkeeper:	*four sets of double letters*
facetious:	*all the vowels in their correct order*
cauliflower:	*contains all the vowels*
education:	*contains all the vowels*

Daily letter race

Challenge children to write in two minutes all the words they can that begin with the first letter of that day of the week.

Word link

Have one child say a word. The next child has to respond by saying a word that starts with the letter that the first word ended with. Make the game more or less challenging by setting a rule determining the minimum number of letters or syllables that the words must have, or require a specific part of speech.

Rule:	*two or more syllables*
First child:	*h*umor
Second child:	*r*ubble
Third child:	*e*lephant

Continuous story

Divide the class into groups. Have one child in each group start a story by saying one word. The next child in the group then adds another word and so on until the group has, word by word, written a story that makes sense. The group that can go on the longest is the winner.

Word Origins

Name _____   Grammar BLM

1. Choose a word from the box to complete each sentence. The Old English root and meaning are given in parentheses.

witness	barrow	ferry	breakfast	grave	scraped

a. I filled the _____ (bera: to carry) with garden waste.

b. I caught a _____ (faran: to go) to take me across the bay.

c. The _____ (witan: to know) testified that she saw the thief.

d. The small boy _____ (sceran: to cut) his knee when he fell.

e. We discovered the old _____ (grafan: to dig) of an explorer.

f. I like to eat cereal and eggs for my _____ (brecan: to break).

2. Choose a word from the box to complete each sentence. The Latin root and meaning are given in parentheses.

city	anniversary	current	manufactured	dentist	errors

a. The strong _____ (curro: I run) swept the swimmers away.

b. The _____ (dens: tooth) extracted my teeth.

c. We celebrate our tenth _____ (annus: a year) next Tuesday.

d. Chicago is a large _____ (civis: citizen).

e. Cars are _____ (manar: a hand) in that factory.

f. Tom made several _____ (erro: I wander) in his spelling.

3. Choose a word from the box to complete each sentence. The Greek root and meaning are given in parentheses.

autograph	astronomer	perimeter	democratic	photograph

a. I took a _____ (photo: light) of our entire grade.

b. The film star gave me her _____ (autos: self).

c. We have a _____ (demos: people) government in the U.S.

d. We measured the _____ (metron: a measure) of the square.

e. The _____ (aster: a star) looked through the telescope.

Root Words

A *root* word is a word from which other words are built.
A *prefix* is a group of letters placed at the beginning of a word.
A *suffix* is a group of letters added at the end of a word.

1. Change the order of the following word parts to make the words suggested by the definitions.

   a. able   un   reason   (not fair)   _____

   b. suit   able   un   (not good enough)   _____

   c. ed   un   want   (not needed)   _____

   d. able   en   joy   (lots of fun)   _____

   e. ly   in   correct   (not in a correct way) _____

2. Circle the root word in each of the following.

   a. unemployment   f. imprisonment

   b. disrespectful   g. disappearance

   c. dishonorable   h. uncertainty

   d. informally   i. reappearing

   e. unpleasantness   j. reconstruction

3. Think of five words of your own that have a prefix. Then think of five words that have a suffix.

Prefix	Suffix

Similes

Name _____ Grammar BLM **76**

A simile is a figure of speech that compares one thing to another. It is a direct comparison introduced by the words *like* or *as*.

1. **Use a word from the box to complete each simile.**

> toast   ice   sugar   mouse   rock   feathers

a. as soft as   _____
b. as sweet as   _____
c. as cold as   _____
d. as hard as a   _____
e. as warm as   _____
f. as small as a   _____

2. **Use a word from the box to complete each simile.**

> silk   bee   kitten   coal   eel   snow

a. The cloth was as black as _____ .
b. The wet ball was as slippery as an _____ .
c. My little sister is as playful as a _____ .
d. The top of this table is as smooth as _____ .
e. I've been as busy as a _____ lately.
f. The lamb is as white as _____ .

3. **Add a word of your own to complete each simile. Compare your answers with those of a friend.**

a. as wet as   _____
b. as big as   _____
c. as graceful as   _____
d. as hot as   _____
e. as tough as   _____
f. as gentle as   _____

Metaphors

A metaphor is more direct than a simile. Instead of saying that one thing is
like **another, it supposes that one thing** *is* **another.**
Simile: *He is as cunning as a fox.*
Metaphor: *He is a cunning fox.*

1. Condense each simile and rewrite it as a metaphor.

   a. All the world is like a stage.

   _____

   b. She was like peaches and cream.

   _____

   c. Fred is like a pig at the table.

   _____

   d. Headlines announcing the crime were like screams.

   _____

   e. Life is like a short summer, and man is like a flower.

   _____

2. Use each word in two sentences—literally in the first, metaphorically in the second.

   a. cloud _____

   _____

   b. forest _____

   _____

   c. river _____

   _____

   d. book _____

   _____

   e. galaxy _____

   _____

   f. snail _____

   _____

Compound Words

Compound words are made up of two or more smaller words.

1. **Add a word from the box to complete each compound word below.**

> ache   knife   proof   quake   prints   coat   where   fly

   a. A severe earth _____ shook the city.

   b. The house is made of weather _____ materials.

   c. Jack always carries his grandfather's pocket _____ .

   d. Tommy has a painful tooth _____ .

   e. We could see the butter _____ in the rose bushes.

   f. We searched every _____ for the missing money.

   g. As it was cold outside, he wore an over _____ .

   h. We could see the foot _____ in the snow.

2. **Circle the compound words. You should be able to find fifteen.**

   Mike got the eggcup from the cupboard and placed it on the clean
   tablecloth. He wanted to eat his breakfast quickly as he was going
   to play football that day. He always played fullback. When he got
   to school, he put his books inside the classroom and then went out onto
   the playground. Everybody asked him if he had remembered to do his
   homework. He said that he had done it in a notebook that
   his grandfather had given him for his birthday.

3. **These compound words have been mixed up. Write the eight words correctly.**

> raindust   carburger   handshoe   eyeprint
> horseshake   cheeseport   sawdrop   fingerbrow

   _____   _____

   _____   _____

   _____   _____

Anagrams

An anagram is a word made by rearranging all the letters of another word.

1. **Rearrange the letters of the word to make a new word to match the meaning in the parentheses. The first one has been done for you.**

   a. sever   (part of a poem)   _____verse_____

   b. sale   (sea creature)   _____

   c. blow   (dish)   _____

   d. seat   (direction)   _____

   e. lump   (fruit)   _____

   f. sore   (flower)   _____

   g. flow   (farmyard bird)   _____

   h. arts   (rodents)   _____

   i. mean   (hair on a horse's neck)   _____

2. **Rearrange the words in parentheses to make more suitable words for the story.**

Tom and his best (lap) _____ Sam were walking through the flower (danger) _____ when they saw a large (low) _____ sitting on the branch of a (lamp) _____ tree. Sam said it (saw) _____ the (seam) _____ one that he had seen (salt) _____ week.

3. **Rearrange the letters of the word in parentheses to make a word that completes the sentence.**

   a. The meal was served on a china _____. (petal)

   b. The _____ is an important organ of the body. (earth)

   c. We put the boxes on the kitchen _____. (bleat)

   d. After heading south, they decided to go _____. (thorn)

   e. The teacher told us to _____. (tinsel)

   f. He hurt his _____ when he jammed it in the door. (fringe)

Synonyms

A synonym is a word that has the same or similar meaning to another word.

1. Circle all the words in the grid. Then write each one beside its synonym.

l	a	r	g	e	t	s
s	l	w	c	r	a	h
o	o	a	l	o	s	a
f	s	i	a	a	t	k
t	e	l	p	m	e	e
s	e	r	i	o	u	s
b	r	a	v	e	r	y

a. howl _____

b. wander _____

c. tender _____

d. tremble _____

e. immense _____

f. misplace _____

g. valor _____

h. applaud _____

i. solemn _____

j. flavor _____

2. Each underlined word can be replaced with a synonym from the box. Find and write the word.

wet	ill	fat	old	odd	gem	sly	get

a. We are trying to <u>obtain</u> some money. _____

b. The <u>crafty</u> fox was captured. _____

c. The clothes are still <u>damp</u>. _____

d. Mary is feeling <u>sick</u>. _____

e. The pig is quite <u>plump</u>. _____

f. This seems quite <u>strange</u>. _____

g. This building is <u>ancient</u>. _____

h. The <u>jewel</u> is very valuable. _____

Antonyms

An antonym is a word that has the opposite meaning to another word.

1. Circle all the words in the grid. Then write each one beside its antonym.

s	b	u	i	l	d	c
m	c	h	e	a	p	o
i	l	e	a	v	e	w
l	t	i	m	i	d	a
e	s	o	u	t	h	r
l	o	o	s	e	n	d
s	w	a	l	l	o	w
a	w	k	w	a	r	d

a. expensive _____

b. bold _____

c. hero _____

d. north _____

e. demolish _____

f. graceful _____

g. tighten _____

h. return _____

i. frown _____

j. spit _____

2. Select the word from the box that has the opposite meaning to the underlined word in each sentence.

solid   divide   smash   light   fake   deceitful   entrance   feeble

a. These books are quite <u>heavy</u>. _____

b. Are you going to <u>repair</u> the motor? _____

c. The teacher told us to <u>multiply</u> the numbers. _____

d. He is a very <u>honest</u> boy. _____

e. We left quickly through the open <u>exit</u>. _____

f. After the operation, she felt quite <u>strong</u>. _____

g. These logs are <u>hollow</u>. _____

h. These diamonds are <u>genuine</u>. _____

Homophones

A homophone is a word that sounds the same as another word but has a different meaning and different spelling.

1. **Circle all the words in the grid. Then write each word beside its homophone.**

f	l	e	e	m	m	g	w
v	f	h	b	e	a	u	a
a	i	y	a	d	y	e	i
i	n	m	w	a	o	s	s
n	d	n	l	l	r	t	t
t	a	u	g	h	t	x	x

a. fined _____

b. ball _____

c. taut _____

d. flea _____

e. meddle _____

f. waste _____

g. guessed _____

h. him _____

i. vein _____

j. mare _____

2. **Circle the correct word in the parentheses.**

Two (buoys boys) were walking beside a (creak creek). They were hoping to (fined find) (sum some) (mail male) (dear deer) that had (been bean) seen grazing on the (berry bury) trees that grew in the vicinity. It was only last (week weak) one had been seen running across the dusty (road rode) (which witch) runs along the side of the forest.

3. **Complete each sentence by using a homophone of the underlined word.**

a. The <u>guest</u> won the prize as she _____ the correct answer.

b. On the packet of self-raising <u>flour</u> there is a picture of a red _____ .

c. My <u>hair</u> stood on end when the _____ ran between my legs.

d. The <u>poor</u> man began to _____ the cold tea into the cup.

e. I watched her <u>peer</u> at the ship as she stood on the _____ .

Homographs

Name _____   Grammar BLM **83**

**A homograph is a word that is spelled the same as another word but has a
different meaning.**

1. **Choose four words and write two sentences for each one. Make sure that each sentence
gives the word a different meaning.**

   (seal   palm   plane   prune   pupil   store   fine   safe)

   a. _____

   _____

   b. _____

   _____

   c. _____

   _____

   d. _____

   _____

2. **Unjumble the letters to make a word that has both meanings in the brackets.**

   a. tje   (plane/spurt of water) _____

   b. rbka   (tree covering/noise of a dog) _____

   c. lcaf   (young cow/lower leg) _____

   d. ewll   (not ill/water hole) _____

   e. rgvae   (serious/tomb) _____

   f. xbo   (container/spar) _____

   g. abll   (plaything/dance) _____

   h. iknd   (caring/type of thing) _____

3. **Think of a homograph that can fill both spaces in each sentence.**

   a. I am sure the money will be _____ now it is locked in the _____ .

   b. The police will _____ you for speeding whether the weather is rainy

      or _____.

   c. Mike _____ angrily when Ben broke the _____ of his bike wheel.

Twin Words

Twin words are words that are often paired together, especially in speech, for example, *salt and pepper*.

1. Add a twin word from the box.

less	sound	there	heels	thin	square	never	down

a. head over _____

b. up and _____

c. thick and _____

d. now or _____

e. safe and _____

f. here and _____

g. more or _____

h. fair and _____

2. Complete each sentence, using a twin word from the box.

take	span	round	nail	again	neck	furious	low

a. The two dogs fought tooth and _____ over the bone.

b. The girls ran round and _____ the yard until they were tired.

c. The room looked spick and _____ after I cleaned it.

d. There has to be some give and _____ if we are to be fair.

e. We looked high and _____ , but we couldn't find it.

f. The horses raced neck and _____ along the course.

g. The match was played at a fast and _____ pace.

h. I have told you again and _____ not to do it.

3. Complete the twin words.

a. fish and _____

b. bread and _____

c. salt and _____

d. hot and _____

e. knife and _____

f. safe and _____

Double Negatives

Name _____   Grammar BLM **85**

If you want a sentence to have a negative meaning, do not put two negatives in it.

Do not say: I <u>didn't</u> see <u>nothing</u>.

Say: I <u>didn't</u> see anything.

   I saw <u>nothing</u>.

Circle the two negative words in these confusing sentences. Then write the sentence correctly to give a negative meaning.

a. I don't want nothing.

_____

b. I can't find nothing.

_____

c. He isn't going nowhere.

_____

d. The new boy doesn't like nobody.

_____

e. I don't want no vegetables.

_____

f. The new principal doesn't know nothing.

_____

g. The children weren't allowed to play no games.

_____

h. I have never read none of those books.

_____

i. We have not been nowhere near the playground.

_____

j. There wasn't none left for me.

_____

Funny Signs

Name _____ Grammar BLM **86**

Briefly explain what is strange about each of these signs.

a. on a bakery window

Homemade cakes—straight from the factory to you

_____

_____

b. on a bakery window

Try our homemade pies—you'll never get better.

_____

_____

c. outside a restaurant

Wanted—young person to wash dishes and two waiters

_____

_____

d. outside a hairdressing salon

Haircuts while you wait

_____

_____

e. at a hardware store

Don't let lawn mowing kill you—let us do it for you.

_____

_____

f. inside a supermarket

Instant soft drink in only 10 minutes

_____

_____

Answer Key

page 14

1.

Clothing	Food
jacket	bacon
trousers	caviar
sweater	biscuits
cap	steak

Body	Sport
knees	yachting
stomach	football
veins	tennis
skull	hockey

2.
a. birds
b. furniture
c. sports
d. vehicles
e. flowers
f. fruit
g. fish
h. dogs

3.
a. thistle
b. walrus
c. zebra
d. apricot
e. stomach
f. planet

page 15

1.
a. skull
b. louse
c. peach
d. trout
e. raven
f. tiger
g. brass
h. pansy
i. onion
j. bread

2.
colored boxes

barrel	hamper
eel	leather
falcon	sofa
silly (opt.)	ferret
pitcher	vinegar
silk	canal
bugle	tall (opt.)
orchid	envelope

3. Answers will vary.

page 16

1.
a. flight
b. batch
c. tuft
d. bunch
e. fleet
f. litter
g. brood
h. library

2.
a. gaggle
b. hail
c. bouquet
d. plague
e. pride
f. staff

3. Answers will vary.

page 17

1.
a. Japan
b. September
c. Henry Hudson
d. Nile
e. Tuesday
f. Miami

2.
Monday
April
Vanessa
Tony
San Francisco
California
Seahawk
Long Beach
Good Friday

3.
a. countries
b. months
c. planets
d. mountains
e. oceans
f. states

page 18

1.
a. journals
b. cities
c. turkeys
d. carts
e. cherries
f. flies

2.
a. loaves
b. chiefs
c. knives
d. halves
e. leaves
f. handkerchiefs
g. thieves
h. wolves

3.
a. armies
b. Dwarfs
c. glasses
d. monkeys
e. oxen
f. ladies

page 19

1.
a. churches
b. trees
c. bushes
d. boxes
e. peaches
f. buses/busses

2.
a. geese
b. men
c. feet
d. lice
e. teeth
f. women
g. children
h. mice

3.
a. potatoes
b. photos
c. volcanoes
d. hippos
e. heroes
f. tomatoes

Answer Key *(cont.)*

page 20

1.
   a. advertisement
   b. marriage
   c. attendance
   d. behavior
   e. decision
   f. encouragement

2.
   a. sadness
   b. bravery
   c. coolness
   d. bitterness
   e. beauty
   f. sickness

3.
   a. punishment
   b. invention
   c. friend
   d. appearance
   e. weight
   f. loss

page 21

1.
   a. the girl's dress
   b. the tiger's stripes
   c. the boy's pencil
   d. the lady's handbags
   e. the tree's leaves
   f. the flower's petals
   g. the clown's antics
   h. the police officer's uniform

2.
   a. the girls' dresses
   b. the donkeys' ears
   c. the men's books
   d. the horses' saddles
   e. the women's houses
   f. the boys' pencils
   g. the birds' nests
   h. the sailors' ship

page 22

1.
   a. fun
   b. pain

   c. health
   d. excitement
   e. length
   f. wealth
   g. happiness
   h. care

2.

abstract nouns

sadness	joy
sorrow	anger
grief	greed
pain	love
fear	glee

3. Answers will vary.

page 27

1.
   a. bit
   b. listened
   c. tapped
   d. read
   e. ate
   f. wandered

2.
   a. gushed
   b. scowled
   c. pounced
   d. wiped
   e. pruned
   f. searched

3.
   a. slithers
   b. gallops
   c. gambols
   d. leaps
   e. struts
   f. waddles

   g. soars
   h. scampers

page 28

1.
   a. constructed
   b. grilled
   c. fell
   d. removed
   e. wrote
   f. performed

2.
   a. draw
   b. obey
   c. throw
   d. quench
   e. comb
   f. burst

3. Answers will vary.

page 29

1.

   at a tennis match

serving	lobbing
acing	volleying

   in the library

researching	reading
studying	browsing

   in the kitchen

roasting	cleaning
peeling	cooking

2.

a. bury	d. stare
b. peer	e. lessen
c. missed	

3.

a. hatch	d. swallow
b. sting	e. jump
c. wash	

page 30

a. talked	d. chatted
b. yelled	e. asked
c. said	f. screamed

2. Answers will vary.

Answer Key (cont.)

page 30 (cont.)

3.

a. bleats

b. gobbles

c. screeches

d. brays

e. grunts

f. trumpets

g. chirps

h. bellows

page 31

1.

a. believed

b. think

c. wondered

d. thought

e. understand

f. enjoyed

2.

a. angered

b. saddened

c. amazed

d. boasted

e. agree/agreed

f. hate/hated

3. Answers will vary.

page 32

1.

a. has   d. was

b. is   e. am

c. are   f. have

2. *underline/circle*

a. going/am

b. painting/is

c. helping/was

d. run/will

e. read/has

f. seen/have

3. Answers will vary.

4. Answers will vary.

page 33

1.

a. thanked

b. barked

c. defeated

d. delighted

e. walked

f. started

2.

a. captured

b. refused

c. wasted

d. whistled

e. described

f. continued

page 34

1.

a. studied

b. denied

c. multiplied

d. buried

e. terrified

f. tidied

g. copied

h. hurried

2.

a. buried   e. terrified

b. multiplied f. tidied

c. denied   g. copied

d. studied   h. hurried

page 35

1.

a. skidded

b. begged

c. dropped

d. robbed

e. knitted

f. stirred

g. traveled

h. dripped

2.

rode	taught
spoke	got
told	ate
brought	went
rang	flew

page 36

1.

a. do make/make

b. did quit/ could control

c. went/did (go)

d. was/could bear

e. did say/smells

f. was /had

2. Answers will vary.

page 37

1.

a. My dog ate a big, hairy spider.

b. The children choose the games.

c. The gardener picks the flowers.

d. Ned kicked five goals.

e. My father crashed the car.

f. The injured dog snapped at the children.

2. (Answers may vary.)

a. Feet should not be placed upon the seats.

b. Your dog should be kept on a leash.

c. Your trash should be put in the bin.

d. No running is allowed.

page 38

1.

a. proved

b. hope

c. behave

d. believe

e. cleaned

f. laughed

2.

a. depart   f. draw

b. enjoy   g. enter

c. collect   h. decorate

d. prepare   i. invite

e. swim   j. govern

Answer Key (cont.)

page 38 (cont.)

3. Answers will vary.

dream
- a. I had a dream.
- b. I dream.

sail
- a. I raised the sail.
- b. I sail.

point
- a. I broke my pointer.
- b. I pointed.

page 39

1. *subject/verb*
- a. dog/is
- b. dogs/are
- c. We/are
- d. I/am
- e. She/runs
- f. They/run

2. *subject/verb*
- a. pack/was
- b. swarm/is
- c. school/was
- d. party/has
- e. team/practices
- f. sack/is

3. *subject/verb*
- a. Mom and Dad/are
- b. bride and groom/come
- c. Sarah and Zoe/are
- d. parents and teachers/meet
- e. Jack and Freya/work
- f. Ned and Max/were

page 45

1.
- a. broad
- b. fragile
- c. circular
- d. childish
- e. perilous
- f. careful

2.
- a. interesting
- b. clever
- c. rusty
- d. delicious
- e. woolen
- f. sunny
- g. ripe
- h. savage

3.

thick	strong
fat	minute
sour	scared
high	big

page 46

1.
- a. fresh
- b. dangerous
- c. deep
- d. false
- e. plump
- f. foolish

2.
- a. peculiar
- b. careful
- c. sudden
- d. serious
- e. sharp
- f. sacred

3.

a. s	e. s
b. o	f. o
c. s	g. o
d. o	h. s

page 47

1.
- a. twelve
- b. two
- c. ten
- d. three
- e. one hundred
- f. fourteen
- g. four
- h. eight

2.
- a. second
- b. first
- c. fourth
- d. fifth
- e. third
- f. sixth

3. Answers will vary.

page 48

1. *adjective/noun*
- a. Those, These/shoes
- b. these, those/tables
- c. That/cow
- d. This/day
- e. Such/silliness

2. Answers will vary.

3.
- a. My; his
- b. Your, our
- c. Their, its
- d. Her, your

page 49

1.
- a. comfortable
- b. dangerous
- c. stormy
- d. patient
- e. valuable
- f. famous

2.
- a. angry
- b. childish
- c. friendly
- d. expensive
- e. cowardly
- f. favorite
- g. furry
- h. hasty

3. Answers will vary.

page 50

1.
- a. Chinese
- b. Welsh
- c. Swiss
- d. Greek
- e. Scottish
- f. French

2.
- a. Turkish
- b. Swedish
- c. British

Answer Key (cont.)

page 50 (*cont.*)
- d. Tibetan
- e. Mexican
- f. Japanese
- g. Italian
- h. Egyptian

3. *adjective/noun*
- a. Turkish/Turkey
- b. Dutch/Netherlands
- c. Irish/Ireland
- d. Norwegian/Norway
- e. Spanish/Spain
- f. Brazilian/Brazil

page 51
1.
- a. oldest
- b. younger
- c. shorter
- d. colder
- e. cutest
- f. smallest

2.
- safest
- wiser, wisest
- paler, palest
- brave, braver
- large, largest

3.
- a. biggest
- b. fatter
- c. saddest
- d. hottest

page 52
1.
- a. busiest
- b. heavier
- c. luckier
- d. noisiest

2.
- a. better
- b. worst
- c. fewer
- d. most

3.
- more beautiful, most beautiful
- luxurious, most luxurious
- more efficient, most efficient
- humorous, most humorous
- delicious, more delicious
- more sorrowful, most sorrowful
- comfortable, more comfortable

page 56
1.
- a. carefully
- b. tightly
- c. brightly
- d. neatly
- e. busily
- f. angrily
- g. softly
- h. gracefully

2.
- a. when
- b. how
- c. when
- d. when
- e. how
- f. when
- g. where
- h. where
- i. how
- j. where

3. Answers will vary.

page 57
1.
- a. there/here
- b. nowhere
- c. somewhere
- d. here/there
- e. below
- f. everywhere
- g. out
- h. inside

2. (Answers may vary.)
- a. heavily
- b. softly
- c. sweetly

- d. swiftly
- e. loudly
- f. slowly
- g. politely
- h. happily

3. Answers will vary.

page 58
1.
- a. peacefully
- b. hurriedly
- c. easily
- d. shortly
- e. tardily
- f. proudly

2. (Answers may vary.)
- a. now
- b. here
- c. punctually
- d. wearily
- e. tonight
- f. tomorrow
- g. tonight/upstairs
- h. noisily

3. Answers will vary.

page 59
1.
- a. feebly
- b. gladly
- c. tidily
- d. foolishly
- e. gently
- f. glumly
- g. abruptly
- h. rapidly

2.
- a. neatly
- b. swiftly
- c. angrily
- d. bravely
- e politely
- f. yesterday
- g. suddenly
- h. later

page 59 (cont.)

3.

a.	o	e.	s
b.	s	f.	o
c.	o	g.	o
d.	o	h.	s

page 60

1.

a. sweetly
b. patiently
c. quickly
d. suddenly
e. gladly
f. poorly

2.

a. easily
b. greedily
c. shabbily
d. clumsily
e. lazily
f. merrily

3.

a. gently
b. comfortably
c. humbly
d. idly
e. feebly

page 62

1.

a. a, a, a, a
b. an, an, a
c. An, a
d. an, a, a
e. an, an

2.

a.	an	f.	a
b.	an	g.	an
c.	a	h.	an
d.	a	i.	a
e.	an	j.	an

page 63

a. an, a, The, an, the, A, the, The,
The, a, a

b. the, the, an, the, An, a, an, an

c. a, the, the, an, a/the, a, an, the,
an, an

page 64

1. Answers will vary.

2.

a. an, an, a, a
b. an, a, a, an
c. a, an, an, a
d. an, an, a, an
e. an, an, a, an
f. an, a, an, a

page 65

1.

a.	a	f.	an
b.	an	g.	a
c.	a	h.	an
d.	an	i.	an
e.	an	j.	an

2.

a.	b.
The/A	an
an	an
an/the	a
a	a/the
a	the
The	the
the	an
the	the
the	the
an	the
the	the
the	a
	a

page 68

1.

a.	from	d.	with
b.	between	e.	under
c.	at	f.	down

2.

a.	beside	d.	around
b.	near	e.	under
c.	against	f.	through

3.

a.	with	d.	of
b.	to	e.	with
c.	on		

page 69

1.

a.	in	d.	down
b.	on	e.	against
c.	across	f.	off

2. Answers will vary.

3. Answers will vary.

page 70

1. *preposition/object*

a. in/park
b. to/farm
c. underneath/table
d. on/lawn
e. through/trees

2.

t	h	r	o	u	g	h
o	f	p	d	w	o	i
v	r	a	o	i	f	n
e	o	s	w	t	f	t
r	m	t	n	h	x	o

a.	over	e.	off
b.	into	f.	from
c.	past/through	g.	down
d.	through/past	h.	with

page 74

1.

a.	she	d.	they
b.	its	e.	her
c.	she/he	f.	him

2. *colored boxes*

we	you
their	my
them	she
they	he
yours	mine
us	

Answer Key (cont.)

page 75

1.
a. his	e. theirs
b. hers	f. yours
c. mine	g. its/his/hers
d. ours	

2.
they	he
their	it
her	mine
she	him

3.
a. Lisa	c. candies
b. Jack	d. sister

page 76

1.
a. my	e. her
b. our	f. mine
c. his	g. its
d. Their	h. ours

2.
a. My, you
b. ours, yours
c. hers, theirs
d. their, ours
e. our, yours

m	i	n	e	h
o	u	r	s	e
y	o	u	r	r
t	h	e	i	r

3. Answers will vary.

page 77

1.
a. Those/adj.
b. This/pron.
c. These/pron.
d. That/pron.
e. These/pron.
f. That/adj.
g. These/pron.
h. That/pron.

2. Answers will vary.
3. Answers will vary.

page 78

1.
a. What/pron.
b. Whose/pron.
c. What/adj.
d. Which/pron.
e. Which/adj.
f. Who/pron.

2. Answers will vary.
3. Answers will vary.

page 81

1.
because
since
when
and
Although
yet
unless

2.
a. salt and pepper
b. knife and fork
c. bread and butter
d. up and down
e. round and round
f. thick and thin
g. fish and chips
h. oranges and lemons

3. Answers will vary.

page 82

1. (Answers may vary.)
a. When we saw the bully coming, we began to run.
b. Because John did not try very hard, he did not pass the test.
c. Unless you help me clean the room, I cannot come out to play.
d. Although it was very hot, we still played soccer.
e. As Tom boarded the school bus, he carried his skateboard.

2. (Answers may vary.)
a. We can do no more until the older boys arrive.
b. Because the tree was not watered, it died last week.
c. Although our best player was missing, we still won the match.
d. Until you behave, I will not give you any candy.
e. Because it hailed last week, the wheat crops were ruined.

page 83

1.
a. since	f. unless
b. because	g. until
c. as	h. although
d. when	i. but
e. and	j. if

2. Answers will vary.

page 84

1. (Answers may vary.)
a. both/and
b. either/or
c. not only/but also
d. Whether/or
e. either/or
f. as/as

2. Answers will vary.
3. Answers will vary.

page 88

1.
a. no	f. yes
b. yes	g. no
c. no	h. no
d. yes	i. no
e. no	j. yes

2. (Answers may vary.)
a. My dog likes to chew bones.
b. Ali picked a rose in the garden.
c. A whale is a mammal.
d. We are going camping this weekend.

3. Answers will vary.

page 89

1. Answers will vary.
2. Answers will vary.
3.
   a. rescued the children from the burning house.
   b. has evaporated.
   c. was discovered in Alaska.
   d. was a famous dancer and actor.
   e. were herded into the yards.
   f. was made of silver.
   g. are found in Egypt.
   h. are native to Australia.

page 90

1.
   a. question
   b. exclamation
   c. command/exclamation
   d. statement
   e. statement
   f. command (request)
   g. question
   h. exclamation
2. Answers will vary.

page 91

1. Answers will vary.
2. Answers will vary.

page 92

1.
   a. Mike tried to rescue his dog from the pool, and he fell in.
   b. John switched on the oven, and he made a cake.
   c. Pam went to the beach, but she did not go for a swim.
   d. Mom cut the lawn, and I raked up the clippings.
2. Answers will vary.
3.
   a. Mike tried to jump the fence/he slipped and fell
   b. Mr. Smith lives in Dallas/ he also has a house in Aspen

   c. Mike and Terry went into the garden/they picked some flowers
   d. You can have a pie/you can have a pizza

page 93

1.
   a. compound
   b. complex
   c. simple
   d. compound
   e. simple
   f. complex
2. Answers will vary.

page 94

1.
   a. "Have you been to New Orleans?" asked Bill.
   b. "Come and help me," shouted Sam.
   c. "The trip was tiring," he said, "I was glad when I arrived."
   d. "It's nearly lunchtime," shouted Mom. "We'll have some fish and chips."
   e. "You can travel all the way by bus," the teacher told us, "and the scenery is beautiful."
   f. Tom said, "We should leave before six o'clock."
2. (Answers may vary.)
   a. Tom said he would like to go on a picnic.
   b. Kate asked where we are going.
   c. Fred asked what time it is.
   d. She said she cannot wait for Christmas.
   e. I asked how far the river is from here.
   f. She asked if they are going with us.

page 96

1. Answers will vary.
2.
   a. in the afternoon
   b. in a frightened manner

   c. in the rear
   d. before noon
3.
   a. in the morning
   b. on the playground
   c. in a cowardly way
   d. before the sowing
   e. with slow carefulness
   f. in the backyard
   g. only a split second

page 97

1.
   a. with long ears
   b. with a guilty conscience
   c. on the old church
   d. on the hill
   e. in the green dress
   f. in the kitchen
2.
   a. aircraft
   b. child
   c. building
   d. house
   e. skyscraper
   f. church
3. Answers will vary.

page 98

1.
   a. to England
   b. with great care
   c. in the box
   d. in an angry way
   e. in my hand
   f. After a short pause
2.
   a. walked
   b. ran
   c. jumped
   d. was working
   e. listened
   f. pushed
3. Answers will vary.

Answer Key (cont.)

page 101

1. *subordinate*
   a. that I read yesterday?
   b. who was arrested by the police.
   c. where the railroad station was.
   d. if we get any hail.
   e. when the snow begins to fall.
   f. because her uncle has arrived.
   g. whose dog bit the policeman.
   h. which has yellow blossoms on it.

2. *main/subordinate*
   a. The student was punished/who stayed away from school
   b. The lady spoke to the teachers/who is in charge of the school
   c. I broke the bottle/that had juice in it
   d. The farm belongs to my uncle/where the grapes are grown
   e. The shed was burned to the ground/that houses the equipment
   f. The cupboard is made of mahogany/that is used to store glasses
   g. The food is in the refrigerator/that is fit to be eaten
   h. We visited the place/where stone is mined

page 102

1.
   a. that killed the sheep.
   b. which began on Easter Day
   c. which was planted in spring.
   d. whose father is from Paris.
   e. that likes to chase its tail.
   f. which is in the museum

2. Answers will vary.

3. Answers will vary.

page 103

1.
   a. can climb
   b. punished
   c. Meet
   d. are going
   e. are allowed
   f. were

2. *clause/action*
   a. because it was hot/why
   b. where there were trees/where
   c. as you wish/how
   d. when the bell rang/when
   e. As our captain is sick/why
   f. where two roads cross/where

3.
   a. until the rain stops.
   b. as if he were very nervous.
   c. because he could not find his uniform.
   d. since she left to live in the city.
   e. even though we will be late.
   f. where the roads meet.

page 104

1.
   a. adjective   e. adverb
   b. noun   f. noun
   c. adjective   g. adverb
   d. adverb   h. adverb

2. Answers will vary.

page 105

1.
   a. I bought the tiger that had black and gold stripes….
   b. The baby who had a pacifier in his mouth….
   c. The teacher who is married with two children….
   d. The train that arrived late….
   e. The bull that has two large horns….
   f. In front of the house which has a red roof….

2. (Answers may vary.)
   a. This is the dog that attacked the stranger.
   b. This is the girl who lives next door to me.
   c. The children hurried past the old house which was said to be haunted.
   d. The big gum tree which stood in our backyard has been cut down.
   e. I knew well the boy who won a silver medal.
   f. The family whose home was destroyed by fire was cared for by friends.

page 106

1.
   a. 3., 4.
   b. 7., 8.
   c. 1., 2.
   d. 11., 12.
   e. 5., 6.
   f. 9., 10.

2. Answers will vary.

page 111

1. *colored boxes*
   Michelle
   England
   Wednesday
   Swan Lake
   Uranus
   Asia
   Shamrock Hotel
   October
   Pacific Ocean
   Easter
   Vietnam
   Christmas
   Canada
   Kansas City
   Murray River
   Mount Everest
   London
   Rialto House
   Wattle Street

2. Answers will vary.

3.
   a. Last Saturday Julie went to Chicago.

Answer Key *(cont.)*

page 111 *(cont.)*

  b. At Christmas we are going to Italy which is a country in Europe.

  c. The wedding will take place at St. Patrick's Church in Greensboro.

page 112

1.

  a. Wheat, rice, and corn

  b. Roses, daffodils, and hyacinths

  c. Skunks, zebras, and penguins

  d. Scissors, pliers, and hammers

  e. Ash, sycamore, and eucalyptus

2.

  a. the capital of South Australia

  b. a Swedish astronomer

  c. a featureless spot in a freezing wilderness

  d. according to a 17th century encyclopedia

  e. one of this class's finest writers

  f. the first international crime fighting organization

page 113

1.

  a. has not

  b. we have

  c. of the clock

  d. did not

  e. we will

  f. cannot

  g. it is

  h. it was

2.

  a. I'm

  b. I've

  c. I'd

  d. I'll

  e. couldn't

  f. you've

  g. who's

  h. it's

  i. he's

  j. weren't

3.

  That's, we'll

  There's

  It's

  We're, you'd

  They're, we've

  They'll, they're

page 114

1.

  a. policeman's

  b. dog's

  c. mother's

  d. clock's

  e. elephant's

  f. child's

2.

  a. ladies'   d. sisters'

  b. children's   e. cities'

  c. cows'   f. eagles'

3.

  a. the horse's ears

  b. the soldier's boots

  c. the men's hats

  d. the tiger's tail

  e. the teacher's books

  f. the clowns' red noses

page 115

1. Answers will vary.

  Examples:

  a. Run! Fire!

  b. Go fast!

  c. Help! Now!

  d. Hold on!

  e. Watch out!

  f. Hurrah!

2.

  a. What a great movie! I really like the end. What big sharks!

  b. Did you see the spider? Look out! There could be one on your hat.

  c. What a lovely day! Look at those waves! Wow!

  d. Yuk! How horrible! Would you believe it!

3. Answers will vary.

page 116

1.

  a. It was nearly Christmas, so we looked for presents.

  b. I was really exhausted; I had never run so far.

  c. Mr. Smith is a good teacher; however, you need to listen to him carefully

  d. Football is a winter sport; baseball is a summer sport.

  e. Lisa was the teacher's first choice; she was quiet, intelligent, and a hard worker.

  f. On our visit to the zoo, we saw zebras grazing in a pen; lots of snakes in the snakepit; seals, their babies, and a diver in the pool; and an elephant in its enclosure.

2.

  a. These are my favorite foods: hamburgers, pies, candy, and apples.

  b. This is what he said, "The United States flag is red, white, and blue." *(or* said:)

  c. Get these things: books, pens, papers, pencils, and crayons.

  d. The instructions read as follows: "Wash lightly in cold water."

3. Answers will vary.

page 120

1.

  a. barrow   d. scraped

  b. ferry   e. grave

  c. witness   f. breakfast

2.

  a. current   d. city

  b. dentist   e. manufactured

  c. anniversary   f. errors

3.

  a. photograph   d. perimeter

  b. autograph   e. astronomer

  c. democratic

Answer Key (cont.)

page 121

1.
   a. unreasonable
   b. unsuitable
   c. unwanted
   d. enjoyable
   e. incorrectly

2.
   a. employ   f. prison
   b. respect   g. appear
   c. honor   h. certain
   d. formal   i. appear
   e. pleasant   j. construct

3. Answers will vary.

page 122

1.
   a. feathers   d. rock
   b. sugar   e. toast
   c. ice   f. mouse

2.
   a. coal   d. silk
   b. eel   e. bee
   c. kitten   f. snow

3. Answers will vary.

page 123

1.
   a. All the world is a stage.
   b. She was peaches and cream.
   c. Fred is a pig at the table.
   d. Headlines announcing the crime were screams.
   e. Life is a short summer, and man is a flower.

2. Answers will vary.
   Example: a. The clouds were gray all day long.
   The clouds were forecasters of the rain to come.

page 124

1.
   a. quake
   b. proof
   c. knife
   d. ache

   e. fly
   f. where
   g. coat
   h. prints

2.
   eggcup
   cupboard
   tablecloth
   breakfast
   football
   fullback
   inside
   classroom
   onto
   playground
   Everybody
   homework
   notebook
   grandfather
   birthday

3.
   raindrop
   horseshoe
   carport
   cheeseburger
   handshake
   sawdust
   eyebrow
   fingerprint

page 125

1.
   a. verse
   b. seal
   c. bowl
   d. east
   e. plum
   f. rose
   g. fowl
   h. rats
   i. mane

2.
   pal
   garden
   owl

   palm
   was
   same
   last

3.
   a. plate   d. north
   b. heart   e. listen
   c. table   f. finger

page 126

```
l a r g e t s
s l w c r a h
o o a l o s a
f s i a a t k
t e l p m e e
s e r i o u s
b r a v e r y
```

1.
   a. wail   f. lose
   b. roam   g. bravery
   c. soft   h. clap
   d. shake   i. serious
   e. large   j. taste

2.
   a. get   e. fat
   b. sly   f. odd
   c. wet   g. old
   d. ill   h. gem

page 127

```
s b u i l d c
m c h e a p o
i l e a v e w
l t i m i d a
e s o u t h r
l o o s e n d
s w a l l o w
a w k w a r d
```

1.
   a. cheap   f. awkward
   b. timid   g. loosen
   c. coward   h. leave
   d. south   i. smile
   e. build   j. swallow

page 127 *(cont.)*
a. light
b. smash
c. divide
d. deceitful
e. entrance
f. feeble
g. solid
h. fake

page 128
1.

a. find
b. bawl
c. taught
d. flee
e. medal
f. waist
g. guest
h. hymn
i. vain
j. mayor

2.
boys
creek
find
some
male
deer
been
berry
week
road
which

3.
a. guessed
b. flower

c. hare
d. pour
e. pier

page 129
1. Answers will vary.
2.
a. jet
b. bark
c. calf
d. well
e. grave
f. box
g. ball
h. kind
3.
a. safe, safe
b. fine, fine
c. spoke, spoke

page 130
1.
a. heels
b. down
c. thin
d. never
e. sound
f. there
g. less
h. square
2.
a. nail
b. round
c. span
d. take
e. low
f. neck
g. furious
h. again
3.
a. chips
b. butter
c. pepper
d. cold
e. fork
f. sound

page 131
a. don't, nothing
   I don't want anything.
b. can't, nothing
   I can't find anything.
c. isn't, nowhere
   He isn't going anywhere.
d. doesn't, nobody
   The new boy doesn't like anybody.
e. don't, no
   I don't want any vegetables.
f. doesn't, nothing
   The new principal doesn't know anything.
g. weren't, no
   The children weren't allowed to play any games.
h. never, none
   I have never read any of those books.
i. not, nowhere
   We have not been anywhere near the playground.
j. wasn't, none
   There wasn't any left for me.

page 132
a. The cakes cannot be both "homemade" and "from the factory."
b. The sign suggests that if ill, one may become even worse after eating the pies.
c. The young person is wanted to wash the two waiters as well as the dishes.
d. Haircuts would have to be done while one "waits" or is present.
e. Let us kill you instead of waiting for the lawn mower to do it.
f. If the drink is "instant," one should not have to wait 10 minutes for it.